Emotional Abuse and Trauma Recovery

Break the Cycle of Manipulation, Heal From Toxic Relationships, and Rebuild Your Self-Esteem

Miriam Sutton

© Copyright 2023 – Miriam Sutton – All rights reserved

The content within this book may not be reproduced, duplicated, or transmitted without direct written permission from the author or publisher.

Under no circumstances will any blame or legal responsibility be held against the publisher, or author, for any damages, reparation, or monetary loss due to the information contained within this book, either directly or indirectly.

Legal Notice

This book is copyright protected. It is for personal use only. You cannot amend, distribute, sell, use, quote, or paraphrase any part, or the content within this book, without the author's or publisher's consent.

Disclaimer Notice

Please note that the information contained within this document is for educational and entertainment purposes only. All effort has been executed to present accurate, up-to-date, and reliable, complete information. No warranties of any kind are declared or implied. Readers acknowledge that the author does not render legal, financial, medical, or professional advice.

Table of Contents

Introduction 4

Chapter 1: Recognizing Emotional Abuse 9

Chapter 2: How Abusers Weaponize Us Against Ourselves ...18

Chapter 3: Trauma Bonding 34

Chapter 4: Breaking Free – Leaving Toxic Relationships...... 50

Chapter 5: Healing Emotional Wounds and Trauma.............. 61

Chapter 6: Rebuilding Self-Esteem 76

Chapter 7: Life After Abusive Relationships 97

Conclusion... 113

About The Author 115

Introduction

History has a funny way of repeating itself. The same is true for relationships. Particularly when it comes to seeking out a partner and the love we think we deserve.

I was sitting with a friend who was very candidly talking about her mental health struggles and the turmoil she was instilling in her then-partner (now-ex).

"His mother is kind of crazy, so he is used to it!"

I nodded absentmindedly, contemplating the situation. She was very self-aware of how she was acting out of sorts and how her behavior came to impact him. At the same time, there lay some recognition in the fact that he, having grown up with a mother who suffered from her mental health issues and soared through turbulent mood swings, was more capable of dealing with his girlfriend.

But what had prompted him to seek out a partner who mirrored the behaviors of his mother? Surely, growing up in a household of chaos, he would have sought a partner who brought him peace and calm; not raised another storm in his adult life.

Yet, these patterns are common. This is not just her story, but mine as well. It took that comment for me to reflect on my own upbringing and how this impacted the partners I was once drawn to.

My father died when I was little, and even before then, love had been a scarcity in my household. As an adult, I shunned boys who suggested reliance and stability. Instead, I was drawn to those who brought me incredible highs followed by desperate lows, who built up my self-esteem then tore it back down again, and who made me work for their love (as if it was ever there to begin with).

It took a long time for me to get over this cycle. We repeat history by seeking out partners who mirror the love (or lack thereof) we experienced as children, both because it is what we have come to know and understand, and also to a degree subconsciously because we think we deserve it, or that we can change it and overcome it – thus healing wounds of the past.

I was already a very vulnerable individual when I entered into my first proper relationship. Still, I came out the other side far more damaged than I had gone in. I took brave steps in opening myself up and sharing my vulnerabilities with someone who had no desire in taking caution with them, but instead weaponized and used my insecurities against me.

It took a long time for me to build myself back up and get to the stage where I am together. Both that relationship and the years thereafter were a lonely time for me. Scarred by the knowledge that some people really will lure you in, build up your trust, and then tear at your weak spots, I was traumatized and put off dating for three years. I educated myself. I built my self-esteem back up. I healed.

Had I not done those things, I would probably still be in the same relationship today. Even if with a different individual. However, I broke the cycle. I hope, in this book, to share with you what I have learned in my journey to spare you the years of loneliness and learning, or hopefully to offer you the courage to leave if you are still in a relationship that is causing you grief.

We all deserve more, even if it is our thoughts or our partner's thoughts telling us otherwise.

My goal is to give you the tools to educate yourself on where you are now, and how you can set yourself free. I know how difficult leaving can be. You feel so entwined with the person causing you the most harm, yet you cannot imagine life without them. You think you can change them. You think you can change yourself to make them happy. But the reality is, you are responsible for no one but yourself. You cannot change people, nor should you.

This book aims to equip you with the tactics to better understand your relationship patterns, your partner's behavior, your own character, and how you can finally build up the courage to leave and then execute that decision.

It might be your husband, wife, or partner. It might be your parent. Perhaps a colleague or neighbor or an old friend. Emotional abuse happens in all forms of relationships. Some of these are not so easy to cut out of our lives, and in these cases, I will still provide you with the tools to set boundaries and protect yourself.

Having picked up this book, I know that you are ready to start your journey toward freedom. You have taken the first step – now is the time to keep reading and educate yourself on how to change your current situation. You are worth more than emotional abuse, and it is time to realize that and set yourself free.

As someone who knows what it feels like to be vulnerable and to have that vulnerability exploited by someone you loved, someone whom you trusted, I know the immense feeling of loneliness that leaves behind. Yet, I have also experienced the gradual realization of my own strength in being able to reclaim my power, educate myself, and work on healing the wounds left behind.

I want you to remember that you are not alone. Even if it may feel like you are in the present moment, countless others have lived through emotional abuse and come out the other side shining. Know that you are not walking this path alone.

In picking up this book, you have already taken the first step toward reclaiming your life. You are deserving of kind love, healthy respect, and happiness – all of which need to come first from within before you invite others into your life to bask in your light.

I have compiled the tools to help you better understand your previous relationship dynamics in comparison to what constitutes a healthy and balanced relationship. Through learning how to detect emotional manipulation, you will be able to identify relationships that only detract from your self-worth, but will also be able to better justify leaving if you are not already at that point.

Additionally, this is not just a book about leaving toxic relationships. It is about rebuilding your self-esteem and sense of worth and discovering who you are and learning to protect your inner self through enforcing healthy boundaries and managing your emotions.

Together, we will recognize, deal with, and heal from emotional abuse, and emerge stronger than ever before.

Chapter 1:
Recognizing Emotional Abuse

"You are so beautiful, just look at you."

I am standing in my boyfriend's bedroom in my underwear, holding his slinky Siamese cat in my arms.

"You are gorgeous."

I am blushing a little bit now. No one has ever called me gorgeous (apart from men in vans driving past with crude wolf whistles).

"You are a 10. Or you would be if you got your tits done."

I still remember that moment very vividly. I felt very beautiful and very seen for a split second, and then it all came crashing down. The aftermath? I was still drawn to my partner. Maybe more so than before. After all, he thought I was beautiful. But I was left feeling self-conscious, crossing my arms over my flat chest.

It did not stop there. He knew I had grown up with an eating disorder, and every so often, he would sprinkle backhanded compliments about my weight or size into the conversation.

"Look at those arms! Getting a little chunky."

"Woah, those shorts are a little tight, right? What a cute belly."

The comments were not just about my appearance either. My (amazing) impression of a Star Wars character was met with a side glance and a frown.

"You are a bit weird." And no, he did not mean that in a good way. It went on. I was too quiet. Too loud. Too closed off. Too clingy. Too independent.

Soon, I did not know myself anymore.

What Is Emotional Abuse?

Emotional abuse is a method whereby individuals try to undermine a person's self-esteem and independence to be able to control and manipulate them to their advantage. It can come in many shapes and forms, such as the following:

Name-Calling and Demeaning Comments: The manipulator frequently uses derogatory language and insults to belittle and demean the victim. They may call them names, and make cruel remarks about their appearance, intelligence, or character, aiming to undermine their self-esteem and assert dominance. These often focus on the manipulator's knowledge of the victim's weak spots and insecurities.

Negging or Patronizing: The manipulator employs a tactic known as "negging," which involves giving backhanded compliments or making condescending remarks to make the victim feel insecure. They may disguise insults as compliments, highlighting supposed flaws or weaknesses in a way that undermines the victim's confidence.

False Accusations: The manipulator frequently makes baseless accusations against the victim, often without any evidence. They may accuse the victim of cheating, lying, or other wrongdoing to create doubt. Through this, the victim feels more compelled to defend themselves or to try harder, to be better for the abuser. This is often a deflection or projection of the abuser's own negative behavior.

Controlling Behavior: The manipulator exercises control over various aspects of the victim's life, such as monitoring their daily activities and tracking their movements, dictating their choices about clothing or activities, or otherwise limiting their freedom. Although a victim might not initially allow for this controlling behavior, they are gradually worn down over time, their self-esteem so impacted that they begin to become eager to please the abuser and do whatever they can to keep the relationship level.

Gaslighting: Gaslighting is a manipulative technique where the manipulator distorts the victim's perception of reality (which we will cover more of in the next chapter). They may deny or minimize their harmful actions, twist facts, and make the victim doubt their memory or sanity. Gaslighting creates confusion and makes the victim feel as if they cannot trust their own judgment, leaving them overly reliant on the person instigating the gaslighting.

Isolating: The manipulator deliberately isolates the victim from their support system, such as friends and family, to gain more control. They may discourage or prevent the victim from spending time with loved ones, telling them that their friends or family dislike them or talk about them behind their back. The end result is that the victim feels dependent on the manipulator for social interaction and emotional support, and has no one else to turn to.

Withholding Affection: The manipulator may withhold love, affection, or intimacy as a form of punishment or control. They may intentionally create emotional distance, giving the victim the silent treatment or withdrawing affection to make them feel unloved and desperate for their attention. The key here is that the affection is here in the first place; manipulators are often experts at giving flattery and affection to give a false sense of security, only to retract it later. This often leaves the victim feeling confused and helpless, as their relationship is sometimes okay. Sometimes more than okay. Sometimes, their partner makes them feel on top of the world. The highs are so good, they begin to forget the lows.

Constantly Starting Arguments: The manipulator instigates frequent arguments over trivial matters, seeking to provoke the victim and keep them on edge. The victim starts feeling like they need to walk on eggshells or repress certain parts of themselves to avoid conflict. They also begin to avoid bringing up areas where they feel unheard or dissatisfied out of fear of starting a huge argument (in which they often end up on the receiving end of blame).

Silent Treatment: The manipulator employs the silent treatment as a passive-aggressive tactic to exert control and punish the victim when they are dissatisfied with them or want to force them to engage in some way. They intentionally ignore the victim, refusing to communicate or respond to their attempts at resolution, leaving the victim feeling anxious, frustrated, and desperate for their attention.

Why Do People Emotionally Abuse Others?

We enter into relationships hoping to find a life partner who will lift us and support us through good times and bad. Why then do some people actively engage in emotionally abusive behaviors? Why do they want to hurt others?

Unfortunately, life is not all sunshine and rainbows. Some individuals enter into relationships with the conscious aim of controlling their partner. This feeling of being in control gives them immense pleasure.

Additionally, children who grew up in households where they were the victim of emotional abuse sometimes grow up feeling the need to exploit others and gain control over those around them as adults, as this is what they were exposed to in their youth. Children who come from unstable households may seek out the instability of an emotionally abusive partner or try to instigate emotional abuse themselves as a way to regain that sense of familiarity.

Am I a Victim of Emotional Abuse?

Whilst individuals who experience a degree of trauma are more prone to entering into emotionally abusive relationships, this is not a one-size-fits-all scenario. You might be sitting there wondering if you were really a victim of emotional abuse since your childhood was perfect and your partner never physically hurts you.

At points, your relationship is perfectly fine. It is pleasant, even. Your partner can be charming to you and those around you. You sometimes wonder if you are housing a Jekyll and Hyde. If that is the case, please do not feel disheartened. Your experience is completely valid.

Some people are however more prone to falling victim to emotionally abusive relationships. In the same way that some partners are more prone to becoming the abuser, others can be more susceptible to falling victim to that abuse.

Factors such as childhood trauma, negative self-worth, mental health issues, or parental influence can leave some people more likely to engage and tolerate a partner who actively hurts them.

Signs of Emotional Abuse

Abusers are often very good at warping our sense of reality through methods such as gaslighting, which we will explore in depth in the next chapter.

Right now, you might well be questioning whether you are actually a victim of abuse, if it is really as bad as it sometimes feels, or if you are just exaggerating things in your head. You see stories about domestic violence or physical abuse and think, my situation is not so bad after all. Maybe I am just being dramatic.

I have thought about this myself on many occasions. The truth is that we lose a lot of ourselves in emotionally abusive relationships when many of us had little sense of self to begin with. If the following red flags resonate with you, chances are you are a victim of emotional abuse.

Understanding these red flags can help you to identify when you are being abused, when to leave a relationship, and how to reach out and get the support that you need.

It is important to note that the presence of one of these red flags is not a clearcut indicator of emotional abuse. However, noticing these types of behaviors continuing to flare up and repeat in your relationship is highly indicative of it.

1. You feel the need to avoid wearing certain types of clothing choices that might anger your partner.
2. Your partner monitors all your messages, social media accounts, or emails.
3. Your partner discourages or prevents you from spending time with friends and family, telling you that your social circle dislikes you and that your partner needs more of your attention.
4. Your partner frequently makes you feel guilty about things, saying that you lead them to act in certain ways.
5. Your partner is excessively jealous and possessive of you, constantly questioning your loyalty or accusing you of cheating or being unfaithful without valid reasons.
6. Your partner regularly engages in belittling or demeaning language, criticizing your appearance, intelligence, or abilities.
7. Your partner consistently dismisses your opinions, needs, or desires. They always prioritize their own preferences and disregard yours.
8. Your partner has your location logged, closely tracks your whereabouts, demands detailed explanations of your activities, or insists on knowing your every move.
9. Your partner gives you the silent treatment, withholds affection, or ignores your feelings as a form of punishment or control when you do enter into disagreements.

10. Your partner seems to always get their own way. They use manipulative strategies such as guilt-tripping, emotional blackmail, or playing mind games. No matter what you do or say, they always have the last word.
11. Your partner holds you to different standards than themselves, imposing rules and expectations that they do not follow themselves. They are incredibly hypocritical; what they expect of you they do not offer in return.
12. Your partner embarrasses or humiliates you in front of others, insults your appearance or intelligence, and deliberately undermines your self-esteem and confidence.
13. Your partner has moved to make you financially dependent on them. They control your bank accounts and prevent you from making independent financial decisions. They scan bills and invoices and scrutinize every purchase you make.
14. Your partner habitually shifts blame onto you, refusing to take responsibility for their actions, mistakes, or shortcomings. If they do seemingly do something wrong, it always turns out to be your fault.
15. Your partner resorts to intimidation, threats, raising their voice, or otherwise acting aggressively in conflict.
16. Your partner consistently ignores or dismisses your boundaries. You feel like they invade your privacy and disregard your personal space.
17. Your partner regularly diminishes or dismisses your feelings, making you feel as though your emotions are unimportant or

unwarranted. You are often labeled as "oversensitive" or "overreacting."

18. Your partner undermines or downplays your accomplishments. Even if you are really proud of something, they laugh it off as trivial and never celebrate how well you have done.
19. If you have children together, your partner manipulates or uses the children as pawns to control or intimidate you. They might try and recruit your children against you or prevent you from seeing them.
20. Your partner uses threats of self-harm or suicide as a means of manipulating your emotions and maintaining control over you. Threatening to leave or calling them out results in these threats, which then causes you to stay.

In this chapter, we have introduced the warning signs and red flags that make up emotional abuse, why abusers act in the way that they do, and who is likely to fall victim to emotional abuse.

Having decided to purchase such a book, I am sure you already had an inkling of the situation you are in. However, I hope you are now confident that in experiencing any of these elements, you are a victim of emotional abuse. Confidence in accepting and acknowledging this position will empower you to better navigate leaving this relationship behind.

In the next chapter, we will explore more of the tactics commonly used in emotional manipulation.

Chapter 2:
Manipulation – How Abusers Weaponize Us Against Ourselves

To emotionally abuse someone successfully, you need to be inside their head, and you need them to trust you. Imagine if someone stopped you on the street today and said, you smell funny and your family does not like you. You would probably laugh it off as a passer-by who maybe needs to lay off drinking, and perhaps take it as a sign to start wearing deodorant.

But imagine a partner, friend, or family member saying these things to you. In the past, you have voiced how you sometimes feel unsettled in your family life. And you have mentioned feeling a bit insecure after someone told you that you smell a little funny as a child. For you, those are soft spots. Weak spots.

Emotional abusers hear these insecurities, organize them away, and save them for later use.

The problem is that how emotional abusers target us often does not leave physical marks or bruises that the outside world can see. Even we may struggle to see the emotional wounds we carry.

"I wish they had hit me, just once."

Weird statement, right? But not uncommon amongst those who have suffered emotional abuse. It is easier to pinpoint physical abuse. I do not want to detract in any way from those who suffer physical abuse – it is equally horrifying and at points more damaging to a person.

However, you can walk away from physical abuse with bruises that prove what has happened. You can show others and explain to them what has happened. You can see for yourself the evidence of what is actually happening.

"I wish they had just been horrible all the time as opposed to giving me glimpses of how good we could have been together."

Another statement that is not uncommonly heard from sufferers of emotional abuse, much for the same reasons as above. Manipulators are great at giving great highs and lows. They can be sweet and adoring and kind when trying to win over a victim, only to then turn to be cruel and controlling. You might build up the courage to leave, and then all of a sudden, you are getting bouquets, gentle shoulder pats, and thoughtful little gestures. How you felt last night, last week, is now moved to the back of your mind. Maybe you start to justify it; "They were just having a bad day. We all have bad days." Or "They have been so kind to me today. It cannot be all that bad."

My ex was wonderful at doing the above. It was almost like he knew my limit. He would push and push me until the very moment I was on the verge of leaving. Then, he would pull a 180 and put on an entirely different character. Criticism would turn into compliments. Silent treatment would be replaced by a constant flow of texts and calls. He would tell me how lucky he was to have me in his life, what a blessing I was. All of those weak spots I had shown him, that he so loved to use against me, he would begin to use to win me back over.

Such is the way of manipulators. Many people who engage in emotional abuse and manipulation qualify as narcissists or have at least some degree of narcissistic personality tendencies.

Narcissistic Personality Disorder

Narcissistic personality disorder (NPD) is a personality disorder whereby individuals have an exaggerated sense of self-importance. They are often considered to be self-centered and lack empathy toward other people.

Common signs of NPD include:

- Having an unreasonably high sense of self-worth and self-importance, often coming across as egoistical
- A constant need for attention, praise, and admiration
- A lack of empathy toward other people, with a general inability to consider the needs of others or how their actions impact those around them
- Feeling like they deserve special treatment or certain privileges
- Excessively boasting about their own talents and achievements, even if they are not as impressive as made out
- A preoccupation with their own physical appearance
- A drive for success and power
- Feeling themselves superior to everyone else
- Criticizing and looking down on other people
- Having no qualms about using people to their advantage
- A lack of self-awareness and inability to process feedback

- Believing that others envy them

Narcissistic Abuse Versus Emotional Abuse

Not all emotional abusers are narcissists. Not all narcissists are emotional abusers. However, there is a strong overlap between the two, as narcissists often possess the emotional intelligence to be able to find people who they can successfully exploit, and then use them to their advantage.

The difference is that narcissistic abuse is instigated by someone with narcissistic personality disorder or traits thereof. This abuse is often intentional. A large portion of a narcissist's personality and drive in life is to seek control over others and manipulate them to their own advantage. This leads to a recurring pattern of manipulative and abusive behavior in multiple relationships in a narcissist's life. Whilst often appearing very charming and magnetic, narcissists are less likely to feel empathy toward others, making it easier for them to manipulate and abuse without feelings of guilt.

By comparison, emotional abuse (not instigated by someone with NPD) may be both intentional and unintentional. It might also occur as an isolated incident or recurrent behavior. Additionally, emotional abusers who do not suffer from NPD or similar traits may be very conscious of the pain they are inflicting. They might have a strong sense of empathy and know how their actions are hurting those around them. They may feel guilty and ashamed, despite continuing to engage in abusive behavior.

Common Manipulation Tactics

Whether you think your partner, friend, or loved one falls under the category of being a narcissist or not, the tactics they use to manipulate and control are often similar. We have already covered a lot of signs and tactics used in emotional abuse to weaken an individual's self-esteem. Below are three larger ways in which abusers work to control and manipulate their victims.

Tactic #1: Love Bombing

Entering into a relationship with a manipulator is often not a slow burn. This is true for partners and friends alike. Things happen very quickly, and whilst being showered with praise and affection feels great, it is worth noting that this is often a strategy used by individuals who are set on gaining someone's trust very quickly.

It is your first date. Second date. Third date. Your date is gushing on about how you are the most beautiful creature on the planet. They have brought you armfuls of expensive and lavish gifts. They have taken you on fancy dinners. They have lightly joked about getting married and what you will call your children. They tell you that they have already told their family about you.

Or you meet a new friend. They tell you that you are fascinating and intelligent and they are so enthralled with your conversation. The next day, they are blowing up your phone with suggestions of meetups and memes and checking in at every hour. You feel thoroughly flattered by how much they seem to think about you.

Or you have just moved into a new neighborhood. Your neighbor drops over a handmade pie and marvels at what a beautiful family you have. You are so lucky, right? They then make a habit of finding an excuse to drop in daily, showering you and your children with compliments and marveling at how they are so lucky to have befriended such a wonderful new family.

Not all niceness is gaslighting, and my aim is not to instill into you fear and suspicion about everyone who pays you a compliment. However, if you are the recipient of an usual amount of attention and flattery, be cautious and consider why this individual is going to such great lengths to win you over.

Tactic #2: Gaslighting

Once an abuser has won over the trust and attention through love bombing and other forms of building trust, the next stage and technique used in successful manipulation is often gaslighting.

Gaslighting is a form of emotional abuse and psychological manipulation. Generally performed over an extended period, the victim comes to doubt their own perception of reality as the abuser intentionally messes with their head.

Types of Gaslighting

Those who actively use gaslighting tend to do so in ways that are not obvious in their methods and often seem unintentional if they do end up offending us or having to explain themselves.

There is also no standard, formulaic approach for how to gaslight. Nonetheless, gaslighting typically involves some of the following aspects:

Lying: We often hear and think of gaslighting as some undercurrent scheme that is hard to detect. However, straight-up lying to your face is not as uncommon as you might think. Even if the abuser knows that the victim will realize that this is a blatant lie, they still engage in it. Whether that is what they were doing on a Saturday night, what they have been spending large amounts of money on, or who they have been messaging. The gaslighter probably knows that you know the answer. Through obviously lying, they create a scenario of betrayal and mistrust. The victim might be left stunned at how easy it was for their partner, friend, or parent to lie, but as the abuser sticks to their guns, they are unable to get past it.

Warping Your Reality: A more subtle manipulation technique is warping the victim's perception of what is and is not real. It is the same as the point above, just conducted more subtly.

For example, you catch your partner flirting with someone whilst you are together at a bar. You call them out, telling them that they acted inappropriately considering you are in a monogamous relationship.

Instead of conceding that they were engaging in flirty behavior (if this is something you have deemed beyond your comfortable boundaries), their response is to deny, deny, deny.

Statements like "That never happened," or "You are making things up," are commonplace in warping a victim's reality.

Even if they are confident in themselves, they begin to doubt whether they are remembering things wrong. Maybe they were just overreacting. Maybe their partner was not being flirty – they were just being kind. As this cycle repeats, the victim begins to lose more of their sense of right and wrong and comes to rely heavily on what the manipulator tells them is right.

Trivializing: Your needs, your wants, your goals – they are not important in the eyes of someone trying to gaslight you. They make their victim feel unimportant, leaving them feeling powerless and more reliant on the abuser. This extends to minor requests a person might bring up, for example, "Please do not say X. I do not feel comfortable with it," in which case the abuser will respond by calling them overly sensitive or telling them they are overreacting. Gaslighting often also extends to bigger goals and dreams. Through making someone feel worthless, they make their victims feel small and insignificant, and more inclined to let the abuser do as they wish as they feel undeserving of anything better.

Scapegoating: So, you have got a gaslighter to fess up to their wrongdoing. You caught them red-handed in a lie. Instead of owning up and admitting defeat and saying sorry, the general response of a gaslighter is to scapegoat. Whatever they did, it is not their fault – it is yours.

In scapegoating, the abuser will blame the victim for their own poor behavior. To do this, they will use what they know about the victim to construct a seemingly sound argument that hits the victim's weak spots.

A good example of this is infidelity. Typically, someone engaging in gaslighting will blame their partner for the infidelity. They might have gone on dating apps, messaged someone, hooked up, and slept over, but it is not their fault. How dare you say that they are to blame for cheating! Owing to your coldness and lack of emotional connection, you drove them to cheat. This is not an issue that they need to be working on at all. Maybe if you were a little more loving, a little more soothing and affectionate, they would not have had to seek that attention elsewhere.

This sounds silly and obvious from the outside looking in. But a victim who already trusts their partner, who has had their insecurities preyed on, and whose very same insecurities are being brought up as the reason for this betrayal will often not see the situation clearly. They will be quick to feel ashamed and will often believe their partner or friend, putting the blame on themselves and feeling guilty for having induced the betrayal.

Coercing: You might have boundaries in place, but these will not be respected by any means. Coercion means encouraging or forcing you to do things that you do not want to do. Or preventing doing things you do want to do. Spending time with family or friends might be off the cards. Engaging in non-monogamous sexual activity, despite you having voiced being incredibly uncomfortable with it, is something you now feel compelled to do as the abuser pushes you past your limits.

Signs of Gaslighting

Gaslighting can come in all sorts of shapes and forms and is so tailored to our sensitivities. It is hard to apply a one-size-fits-all formula to demonstrate gaslighting, but if you think that some of the below statements relate to your relationship, there is a high chance that you are on the receiving end of gaslighting and emotional abuse.

- They consistently tell you that you are overly sensitive and that your emotions are exaggerated or invalid.
- They frequently twist your words and reinterpret conversations to make it seem like you said something you did not or meant something different.
- They accuse you of being paranoid or crazy whenever you confront them about their behavior.
- They often use subtle put-downs or sarcasm to undermine your self-esteem and make you doubt your worth.
- They insist that they have your best interests at heart, but their actions consistently contradict their words.
- They frequently bring up past mistakes or vulnerabilities to make you feel guilty and keep you on the defensive.
- They isolate you from friends and family by making negative comments about them, causing you to question your relationships.
- They insist that you are the one with the problem and that they are just trying to help you see the truth.
- They accuse you of imagining things or making things up, even when you have evidence to support your claims.

- They often deny promises or agreements that you distinctly remember them making.
- They use gaslighting techniques to make you doubt your attractiveness or desirability, causing you to become overly dependent on their validation.
- They make you doubt your competence and capabilities, undermining your confidence in areas where you once excelled.
- They selectively bring up past events or conversations to distort the narrative and make you question your own memory.
- They frequently play mind games, using manipulation tactics to keep you off balance and unsure of what is real.
- They insist that everyone else is lying to you or conspiring against you, except for them.
- They often downplay or dismiss your achievements or successes, making you feel inadequate and unworthy of praise.
- They twist conversations to make you feel guilty for their own mistakes or wrongdoings.
- They consistently break boundaries and invade your privacy, then gaslight you by denying or downplaying their actions.
- They use gaslighting as a way to control your financial resources and make you dependent on them.
- They engage in manipulative behavior and then blame you for their actions, making you feel responsible for their choices.

Tactic #3: Triangulation

An additional method of manipulation and control used by abusers is the introduction of a third party. The name is a giveaway; at the top sits the abuser. Below, are two other individuals (or maybe a pet). Whoever is at the top obviously holds the most control.

In triangulation, a sense of rivalry and competition is brought into play. You feel like you have to compete for the affection of whoever is atop the triangle. The abuser's goal is to create a sense of insecurity and competition. If you feel like you are not winning, you work harder.

Emotional triangulation exists perhaps most obviously in romantic relationships. I for one did not notice this until the end of my relationship.

My ex had a female best friend.

Naively, I was happy for him. In my eyes, being so close to a girl meant he would understand me better. I do not want to instill the stereotypical fear that you should never trust your partner's best friends, but for me, the stereotypical outcome played out.

She was blonde and buoyant, permanently tanned, and good at doing her makeup.

Suddenly, little comments popped up from my partner.

I, a dark brunette, should consider dying my hair platinum.

How about I fake tan a bit more?

Why not wear a bit more makeup?

And yes, her fuller-sized chest also came into play.

The competition he created was not obvious. It was little comments thrown in here and there. She was fun and energetic. They had spent such a great time at the weekend together. He had helped retrieve her car after it had been towed. They had such a longstanding history together. But I was not to worry – they were just friends after all.

I opened Snapchats from him, that she had taken (of herself ... looking back, I am not quite sure how I missed the signs) and smiled to myself, content that he was enjoying his time with his best friend.

I say this to demonstrate the naive extent to which triangulation can slip under your nose. A part of me was subconsciously jealous and concerned, my insecurities aflame at all of his little comments comparing me to his best friend. The other part of me was just really gullible and truly believed that his best friend made him happy, so I should be happy and embracing too.

Triangulation does not exist only in romantic relationships. You might also find that a parent pits you against your siblings when it comes to competing for their affection. A best friend might induce a situation where you feel like you are constantly in competition with best friend 2 for the prime spot (and no, you cannot all get along equally – it does not work like that in the gaslighting world).

In some weirder situations, pets also get brought into the mix. Narcissists and abusers can put on a big show of love for their animals, treating little Pomeranians like princesses and showering huskies with adoration, and then treating their partner with cruelty and coldness.

The Impact of Manipulation on Victims

We have covered some aspects of how abusers seek to control and manipulate their victims.

What impacts do these forms of emotional abuse have, apart from having the victim under their thumb? The long and short-term impacts of emotional abuse will be covered in Chapter 5, but for now, here are some typical impacts of emotional manipulation that many victims experience:

Doubt and Confusion: Victims often find themselves doubting their own perceptions, memories, and judgments. They may question their reality and constantly second-guess themselves due to the manipulator's gaslighting tactics.

Low Self-Esteem: Emotional abuse chips away at victims' self-worth. Constant criticism, put-downs, and comparisons can erode their confidence, making them feel unworthy, inadequate, or unlovable.

Isolation: Manipulators often isolate victims from friends, family, and support networks, creating a sense of dependency and making it harder for victims to seek help or escape the abusive situation. This isolation can further contribute to victims' feelings of loneliness and helplessness, as they feel like the only person they can rely upon is the person causing them this distress (although they may be unaware of this).

Emotional Distress: Victims may experience a range of negative emotions, including anxiety, depression, fear, and constant stress.

The emotional roller coaster created by the manipulator's tactics can lead to emotional instability and mental health challenges.

Loss of Identity: Victims of gaslighting and other forms of emotional abuse may lose touch with their own wants, needs, and desires as they adapt their behavior and preferences to please the manipulator and avoid conflict. Hobbies or interests they previously enjoyed might be trivialized and deemed stupid, meaning they refrain from pursuing things they truly enjoy.

Guilt and Self-Blame: Manipulators frequently shift blame onto their victims, making them feel responsible for the abuse, for not meeting the manipulator's expectations, or for the manipulator's poor behavior. Victims may internalize this blame, leading to feelings of guilt, shame, and stress, all of which negatively impact self-esteem.

Difficulty in Trusting Others: After experiencing emotional abuse and manipulation, victims may find it challenging to trust others. This lack of trust can impact new relationships or friendships, leaving them unable to build up new support networks during or after the abusive relationship.

Boundary Issues: Manipulators often disregard personal boundaries, making victims question their own boundaries. The effect is that victims struggle to establish and maintain healthy limits in relationships. They may have difficulty in recognizing and asserting their own needs going forwards, and be prone to people-pleasing. They may create rigid boundaries which prevent new individuals from entering their lives and building new connections.

Self-Doubt and Indecisiveness: Constant manipulation and control can leave victims feeling incapable of making decisions or trusting their own judgment. They may become overly reliant on the manipulator for validation and guidance, losing confidence in their ability to make choices independently.

Post-Traumatic Stress Symptoms: Victims of severe emotional abuse may develop symptoms similar to those seen in post-traumatic stress disorder (PTSD). Flashbacks, hypervigilance, nightmares, and emotional reactivity can occur as a result of the trauma endured.

Post-Betrayal Syndrome: Someone in your close circle violating your trust can have a lingering effect and cause long-term trauma which involves emotional distress and an inability to trust others out of fear of experiencing another betrayal.

In this chapter, we have explored emotional abuse tactics in greater depth. You are likely better informed as to what would construe a sweet gesture, what is love bombing, and can list off with confidence the occasions where your abuser has weaponized your insecurities against you.

In the next chapter, we will be covering why we return to those who hurt us, how trauma bonds arise, and how to break such a bond.

Chapter 3:
Trauma Bonding

Why We Return/Stay With Those Who Hurt Us

You would think that naturally, we would run from things that hurt us. Prey run pretty fast when chased by natural predators. You do not tend to find baby zebras running into the mouths of lions, especially if their mothers just got eaten ...

So why is it that we often return to relationships with abusers?

Unfortunately, my experience was no different. I am not proud of it, but after being love bombed, gaslit, and cheated on, I still went back. More than once. Over a period of several years.

Each time, he told me he had changed. He had grown. He had realized the error of his ways and how badly he had treated me. He realized how much he had lost and wanted to prove to me how much he had changed. I was so deserving of more, I was the best thing that had happened to him, and could I not just let him show me quite how much he was capable of?

(I want to precursor this by saying this is not universal. People can change. Some will, some will not. Just do not be tempted to fall for false gestures and grand claims when you know the person, deep down, remains the same).

Personally, every time, I fell for it. I looked at him and I saw the good. My mind glossed over the days and nights I had spent sobbing alone in bed and instead stuck to the good memories we shared. I embraced his excuses and clung to his false promises and was more than ready to welcome him back with open arms.

And so the cycle repeated, again and again.

The cheating and the gaslighting never stopped. Each time he came with a new or tailored excuse, and continued to cheat and chip away at my self-esteem.

So why did I go back? Why after the first time, had I not learned my lesson? After all, the saying goes "Make a mistake once and it becomes a lesson. Make a mistake twice and it becomes a choice."

I do not like this quote as I think that for recipients of emotional abuse, navigating choice when it comes to returning to abusers is a more nuanced and complex subject. This errs on victim blaming, although I understand completely why those on the outside looking in would think that we are choosing the behavior we receive in staying in relationships or returning to abusers.

If you have repeatedly returned to an abuser and think this applies to you, you are not alone.

Trauma bonding is a pretty regular occurrence in abusive relationships. It is the connection that bonds the abuser to the abused and creates a form of attachment through negative abuse patterns followed by positive reinforcement and encouragement. More commonly known as highs and lows. A form of addiction, if you like.

Whilst you might want to run from your predator, you often forget how bad it is when it is bad. Rose-tinted glasses leave the victim unaware or unwilling to see quite how badly they are being treated, so they continue to return to the abuser. Additionally, these constant highs and lows create a sense of constant stress coupled with dopamine when the abuser does treat you well. You become addicted to that emotional frenzy and dependent on the abuser.

Trauma bonding happens not only in personal relationships. It is also prevalent in children toward abusive parents, in cult members and their leaders, and in hostages and kidnappers (a form of Stockholm syndrome).

Trauma bonding generally occurs in abusive relationships where the abused are provided with certain highs. It is often easier to leave if you are constantly being mistreated. However, if the abuse is coupled with affection and tenderness, it is less easy to justify leaving.

On top of that, dependency on the abuser is a big cause of constantly returning to their presence. Having isolated yourself from your friends and family, you feel as if you have nowhere else to go and no one to turn to. Old memories of yourself, your previous life, and your sense of identity also begin to become clouded. Your identity gradually becomes wholly dependent on the abuser, making life without them seem very difficult to imagine. Who would you even be without them?

Love bombers can also make you feel on top of the world. Calling you their soulmate, the light of their life, and the apple of their eye (in the good times), you glow with excitement at the thought of being so cherished. How could you ever let someone go who insinuates that they love you so much and make you feel so very special?

Signs You Are in a Trauma Bond

It can be difficult to discern when you have managed to get yourself into a trauma bond. We often lose perspective of the wider picture and struggle to see beyond the confines of the relationship and individual we are bound to. Below are some signs to help you identify whether or not this applies to you:

- You may find yourself feeling consistently unhappy and dissatisfied in the relationship, and you might even lose attraction or affection toward your partner. Despite this, you feel trapped and unable to leave.
- When you attempt to break free from the relationship, you experience intense emotional distress. The thought of leaving causes anxiety, fear, or even panic, making it extremely challenging to commit to leaving.
- Your partner may make promises to change when you express your desire to leave and promises you the world, but they never actually end up following through with what they say.
- You tend to fixate on the positive aspects of the relationship, especially the rare moments of kindness, love, or affection. You use these instances as evidence that your partner truly cares about you and you tend to blindly overlook the negative aspects.

- You consistently blame yourself for the abuse and believe that you are the cause of the problems in the relationship. You may feel unworthy of love or believe that you deserve the mistreatment, further deepening the trauma bond.
- As the trauma bond intensifies, you may find it increasingly difficult to maintain your personal boundaries. You might tolerate behavior that goes against your values or allow your partner to disrespect you or your beliefs without even thinking about speaking up.
- The fear of retaliation or punishment from your partner prevents you from taking steps to end the relationship or seek help. You find yourself walking on eggshells in their presence to avoid any conflict.
- When other people express concern about your partner's behavior or raise questions about the healthiness of the relationship, you find yourself making excuses for your partner or defending their actions. You may downplay or rationalize the abuse, believing that they did not mean it or that they are capable of changing.
- Despite the mistreatment and abuse, you continue to trust your partner and hold onto the hope that they will eventually change or turn back into the initial love bomber they showed you in the beginning. You may believe that your love and support will be enough to transform them into a better person, leading you to stay in the relationship with the expectation of improvement.

- You protect your partner by keeping their abusive behavior a secret. You may feel ashamed or embarrassed about the abuse, fearing judgment or disbelief from others. As a result, you suffer in silence and avoid seeking help or support.

Susceptible Individuals to Trauma Bonding

There is no clear cut between who is more likely to fall into a trauma bond. People with negative self-worth may be just as likely targets as confident and independent thinkers. Some narcissists and abusers will purposefully seek anxious and easily attached individuals to break them down, identifying those who lack a strong support network or who feel insecure about themselves.

Equally, they might seek out independent thinkers and confident individuals and gain a higher sense of self-worth and control in manipulating those with high self-esteem, whom you might not think otherwise susceptible to emotional abuse.

However, a few notable risk factors for those who might be susceptible to experiencing a trauma bonding include:

- People with anxious or avoidant attachment styles
- People with dependent personalities who seek out relationships to feel valued and loved
- People with separation anxiety
- People who fear rejection or abandonment
- People who experience self-doubt or have a negative sense of self-worth

- People who experienced childhood abuse or abuse in previous relationships
- People with pre-existing mental health conditions such as BPD, anxiety, or depression
- People with an inherent forgiving nature who seek to see the "good" in everyone and are naive in overlooking abuse

The Stages of Trauma Bonding

The stages that precursor a trauma bond are similar to many of those covered in the previous chapters. However, to briefly summarize, emotional abuse in relationships tends to come in the following stages; the end result for many is a trauma bond with their abuser.

1. **Love Bombing:** an intense degree of flattery and compliments. The recipient is showered with affection intensely over a brief period, making them fall quickly for the abuser and feel unique and special.
2. **Building Trust:** After an initial shower of affection, the abuser moves heaven and earth to gain the victim's trust. They rush into premature commitments such as moving in, getting married, or doing major acts of service to prove their worthiness and create a sense of dependency.
3. **Criticism and Degradation:** Once trust has been built, the abuser begins to lightly criticize and degrade the victim. This might seem minor and unnoticeable at first. Small comments may be made regarding appearance or intellect, and the abuser demands more and more attention whilst never

seemingly being pleased with what you can provide them. Already dependent on their attention, you begin to work harder to please them, even at the cost of yourself.

4. **Gaslighting and Manipulation Tactics**: The abuser begins to warp your sense of reality by calling you sensitive or saying factual events never even happened. The trust and dependency that has been built up mean that you do trust what they say, even despite minor concerns or doubts in your head. Often, the victim comes to blame themselves for everything they are accused of, even if they had no part in it.

5. **Loss of Identity and Isolation:** With the abuser likely having encouraged you to push your friends and family away, you lose any form of support network that might have been able to convey the true nature of the situation. On top of that, you experience a loss of identity. Your boundaries are broken and you feel constantly exhausted in attempting to even justify yourself or fight back. Any sense of self-worth has also been damaged, leaving you feeling worthless and at a loss without the company of the abuser.

6. **Resignation and Submission:** Even an attempt at discussing behavior or boundaries with the abuser results in gaslighting and criticism, so you begin to refrain from even trying as it has such a hard impact on your sense of self-worth. You walk on eggshells around the abuser to avoid conflict and try your hardest to please them, desperate to return to the initial self they presented in the first stages of the relationship. Fleetingly, this affection and praise do return, giving you hope

that you can regain a healthy relationship. However, any highs are quickly followed by a deep dive into criticism and gaslighting; forming a circular pattern.

7. **Trauma Bond:** Desperately stressed and anxious at all times, you crave the brief periods in which you feel loved and worthy. So despite the abuse and degradation, you keep going back. The emotional highs of your relationship become addictive and little else brings you the pleasure of pleasing your partner in those brief moments.

How to Break Free From a Trauma Bond

Trauma bonds are a form of addiction, which is not easy to break. However, I, amongst many others, have managed to do so. It is not an easy process. It takes a great deal of self-reflection on your current status and what your relationship is like in reality, coupled with effort and resilience in breaking away. Just remember: Many other people have felt like they are in the same situation. They have felt hopeless, attached, alone, broken, defeated. And yet, they have come out the other side shining. If this applies to you, you have the power and strength in you to break free from the trauma bond to your abuser.

Educate Yourself on Abuse and Trauma Bonds: If you have doubts about whether or not you are the recipient of abuse, hopefully, this book has provided you with plenty of red flags and signs to look out for. However, do not stop there. I have listed some comparisons between a healthy relationship and an unhealthy relationship below. Compare the two for a better idea of where you sit.

Take a Step Back to Reflect: You do not have to leave just yet (we will get to that), but try to find some space and take a step back to truly reflect on how your experience has been in your relationship. Write lists of things you have felt and experienced and have a tough and honest look at patterns that may be repeating themselves.

Find a Support Network: This one is tricky as an abuser's tactics often involve isolating the victim from loved ones, but where possible, reach back out. Reconnect with family and friends – you will be surprised how much people are willing to welcome you back. Failing that, support groups online provide plenty of support and advice as well as communities for victims of emotional abuse.

Look After Yourself: Breaking free from a trauma bond means building your sense of self-worth and identity back up. To do so, practice self-care. Try and incorporate more of the activities and hobbies you loved and be ready to try new experiences. Mindfulness, journaling, exercise, meditation. Anything that makes you feel good will help restore your strength to break free.

Envision Your Ideal Future: Even if you seem lost in the present, envision what your ideal future looks like. What is your lifestyle like? Who do you surround yourself with? Who are your friends and family? What does a day in your life look like? Keep that idea in mind to empower you to break free from your present situation.

Be Ready for the Long Road to Healing and Recovery: Healing does not happen overnight. However, remind yourself that you are worthy of happiness and enjoyment. You do not deserve to be controlled or degraded in any way. Remind yourself of your worth and remind yourself that you do not need someone else to make you happy; you alone are more than capable of finding happiness for yourself.

Consider Therapy: If this is available to you, consider working with a professional to assist you in breaking your trauma bond and reflecting on your situation, as well as developing a path for the future.

As basic as these points might be, using what constitutes a generally healthy relationship to compare to elements of unhealthy relationships or trauma bonds can be useful as a bit of a wake-up call if you are having doubts or you think that it is just "not bad enough."

Healthy Relationships

- Honesty and trust
- Mutual respect
- Respected and healthy boundaries
- Active communication
- Willingness to take responsibility for one's actions
- Lifting each other and supporting one another

Unhealthy Relationships/Abuse/Trauma Bonds

- Emotional abuse
- Isolation
- Criticism and degradation
- Threats and intimidation
- No consideration of boundaries

- Lack of trust
- False accusations

Relationship Assessment Quiz

Consider the following questions when reflecting on your relationship with that person. Be honest – you have got no one to hide your true feelings from.

1. Do you feel respected and valued by your partner?
2. Are you able to openly communicate your thoughts and feelings with your partner without fear of judgment or retaliation?
3. Does your partner ever react in ways that you find alarming or scary?
4. Does your partner support your goals, dreams, and personal growth?
5. Are disagreements and conflicts in your relationship handled respectfully and constructively?
6. Do you have a healthy balance between time spent together and time spent apart?
7. Do you feel comfortable being yourself around your partner, without having to put on a facade or pretend to be someone you are not?
8. Do you ever feel like your partner has a temper or is not in control of their emotional reactions?
9. Does your partner encourage your autonomy and independence?

10. Do you have a sense of trust and security in your relationship?
11. Do you ever feel like your partner tries to wind you up or push your buttons?
12. Are you able to set and maintain boundaries with your partner, and do they respect those boundaries?
13. Does your partner take responsibility for their actions and apologize when they have hurt you?
14. Do you feel supported by your partner in times of need or difficulty?
15. Are you able to pursue your own interests and maintain relationships outside of your romantic partnership?
16. Does your partner show empathy and understanding toward your emotions and experiences?
17. Do you feel safe and physically and emotionally secure in your relationship?
18. Do you ever feel like you take the blame for all disagreements and conflicts, even if you do not truly feel like it was your fault?
19. Are you able to express your opinions and make decisions together as equals?
20. Does your partner encourage your self-care and well-being?
21. Are you able to freely express your concerns or raise issues without fear of retaliation or punishment?
22. Do you feel a sense of happiness, joy, and fulfillment in your relationship?
23. Do you ever feel unsafe around your partner?

24. Does your partner support your emotional well-being and encourage you to seek help when needed?
25. Do you feel a healthy balance of give and take, where both partners contribute to the relationship?

After answering the questions, count the number of "Yes" and "No" responses.

If you answered mostly "Yes," this suggests you have a healthy relationship where both partners respect, support, and communicate effectively with each other.

If you answered a mix of "Yes" and "No" responses, this may indicate an unhealthy dynamic in certain aspects of your relationship. Consider communicating these issues to your partner and a professional therapist if required, and be cautious of how far unhealthy extends to emotional abuse.

If you answered mostly "No" responses, this may indicate a potential trauma bond or an emotionally abusive relationship. It is crucial to remain candid and aware of the reality of what you are experiencing and the extent to which this relationship is impacting your life and your self-worth. Where possible, seek guidance from a professional therapist to assist you in navigating the next steps.

Trauma Bond Versus Codependency

Codependency is another element that can often arise in relationships where one or both parties depend heavily on the other. Whilst not the healthiest approach to forming relationships, it can differ from trauma bonds. Victims may well be codependent on their abusers, but couples can also experience codependency without emotional manipulation or abuse.

In codependent relationships, one person tends to rely on the care and attention of the other. Abuse may well not be present, but the codependent party still suffers anxiety and requires constant reassurance to feel safe.

Codependent partners may often be "attached at the hip," with the codependent partner ignoring their own needs to cater to their partner at all costs.

Final Words

Remember, you are stronger than you realize. It is time to break free from the trauma bond that has held you captive. Embrace your worth and know that you deserve a life filled with joy and freedom.

With the newfound knowledge this book has given you, you should be able to see the bond that binds you to your abuser more clearly and understand the reasons behind it. You are never to blame for the bind that pulls you back to your abuser.

Educate yourself and reflect on your relationship, seek support from those who can lift you and give you strength. To break this bond, you need to believe in yourself and the future that is very much within your grasp.

Liberation awaits, and you have the strength to seize it – as we will cover in the next chapter.

In this chapter, we have covered what trauma bonding is and how it arises in emotionally abusive relationships. If you were repeatedly returning to a friend, partner, or parent who hurt you and did not understand why you just kept going back, hopefully you now better understand, but also have the tools to begin breaking free.

In the next chapter, we will be covering how to physically break free from an emotionally abusive relationship in a safe manner.

Chapter 4:
Breaking Free – Leaving Toxic Relationships

O nce that trauma bond is broken (or maybe it is not even broken yet, you have just decided to leave. You might leave and return. Such is part of the process of leaving emotionally abusive relationships), you then need to work out how you are actually going to set yourself free.

Physically leaving can be incredibly difficult if you live a life solely reliant on your abuser and find yourself isolated from your family, or if you are very attached to whomever you have this relationship with, whether it is a romantic partner, family member, colleague, or friend, and for whatever reason will struggle to create distance.

The bravery it takes to finally exit an emotionally abusive relationship is paramount, and if this is a decision you have come to, I want you to remind yourself how courageous this step is. Deciding to leave is incredibly brave. Whilst it is daunting, you are not alone in this process.

Choosing to leave and not look back is one of the things I am most proud of. Looking back, it is a decision I wish I made sooner – but life cannot be composed of wistfulness and what-ifs.

In itself, choosing to leave and committing to creating distance in emotionally abusive relationships is a step many never get to take.

The path to rediscovering who you are beyond the confines of an emotionally abusive relationship, whether a parent, friend, or partner, can be daunting.

But it is not a path you need to travel alone. Nor are you the first person to venture down this path; the below tools are some that I have compiled through my own experiences, which will be useful in helping you to plan and enforce how you deal with leaving behind an abuser.

Your Exit Strategy

As in physically abusive relationships, safety remains a priority when actually leaving a relationship or creating distance between yourself and the abuser. If you think you are at all at risk of any threat, reach out to the relevant authorities.

However, if leaving is unlikely to put you in harm's way (despite being a difficult decision), consider the following when actually implementing your exit and reminding yourself not to go back.

Reflect on Your Emotions: Hopefully, the previous chapters have provided you with more clarity on what constitutes an abusive relationship and have reassured you that what you are going through is not what you deserve, if relevant to your situation.

Sit with this knowledge, and where possible, write down your feelings and experiences.

- How happy have you truly been in this relationship over the past few months/years?

- Have you felt held back or limited in any way by this person's presence?
- Has your sense of self or your identity changed whilst you have been in a relationship with them?
- Has your emotional state been impacted by their presence?
- Do you think that being in a relationship with them has impacted other relationships you previously had?

Even if you can acknowledge the negative impact someone leaves on your life, it can be difficult letting them go out of guilt.

Referring back to the friend I mentioned at the start of this book, she is someone I chose to let go of as well. Although she brought me great highs and we enjoyed fantastic moments together, we were deeply bonded over our shared mental health issues, mainly related to eating disorders. There came a point where these issues no longer breached my life, yet continued to wrangle hers.

Also diagnosed with BPD, she grew more unwell as I grew better and grew increasingly frustrated with how I seemed to let go of my own mental health struggles.

The decision to let go of our friendship still cripples me. Whilst I would not classify her as a narcissist or abuser by any means, it took tremendous difficulty for me to put myself first and decide when her influence on my life was having too negative an impact.

As I grew past my eating disorder, she would belittle my progress and tell me, in short, that I was not well. She would threaten suicide and self-harm, and say I was the only person she had left.

Having also supported her through drug addiction, my other friends grew increasingly concerned for my well-being. Supporting someone who threatens to self-harm if you cannot support them correctly is a great burden to bear.

So, we came to part ways. It is still a sore spot in my heart and I hope she is doing incredibly well, but in this, I learned that although putting yourself first feels immensely selfish, it is necessary. In truth, there are a few occasions where you should not be putting yourself first.

So hopefully you can reflect on how much damage someone is doing to you and can empower yourself to realize that in life, your life alone is the one you need to bear responsibility for.

Letting people go can be heart-wrenching, but when they bring us sorrow and do us damage, it is a necessity.

Be Honest With Yourself: Following on from the above, try where possible to take off those rose-tinted glasses. A great deal of being in a relationship with an abuser means lying to those around you, as well as (and more importantly) to yourself.

I was fine, I told myself, as I took my third anti-anxiety pill at 3 AM after my boyfriend had not replied for three days. I was fine, I told my mother after she heard my silent sobbing at night. It is fine, it was not his fault, I told my friends after I came home from the sexual health clinic with results that you really should not be getting 8 months into a monogamous relationship.

Are you actually fine? Are the highs really better than the lows?

I can probably answer that question for you and tell you that they are not.

The few glimpses of sunlight amongst the shadows are not worth a lifetime of clawing through the clouds to try and find them. Beyond those clouds lies a life where it can be sunny all the time. Or at least for the most of it.

So be honest with yourself. Call out any little voices in your head that tell you otherwise, that justify your abuser's behavior, that try and tell you that they need you, that it is not so bad, that others have it worse, that sometimes it is fine.

Sometimes, it can be hardest to expose our own lies, to ourselves. But the tougher and more honest you are, the more you will feel empowered to leave and not look back.

Reach Out to Friends and Family: The road to healing after leaving an emotionally abuse relationship is long and is a path best walked with the company of others.

Whilst abusers often isolate us and you might be thinking, there is no one left for me to call – you would be surprised. I certainly was.

"How are you …"

My sheepish texts sent out to my best friends, whom I had not spoken to in months and whose presence I had shunned over my ex's presence were quickly answered. Within minutes, actually.

Turns out, they did not hate me in the way he had told me they did. They had been very worried about me. And they were more than ready to embrace me with open arms when I decided to leave.

Depending on your abuser, the people you turn to might differ. You might be turning away from family members to friends. Or from certain friends to other friends. Or to support networks, in person and online, if that is more convenient for you.

Whatever the situation, give reaching out a go. Often, our loved ones can see the situations in play more clearly than we can.

My friends and family knew what was happening to me. They knew they could not change my mind nor force me to leave – they could only wait until I was ready.

So when that time came, they welcomed me with open arms and were there to help me through my doubts and worries, building my self-esteem back up.

Physically Leave: Make sure you have a safe place to go if you share a residence with your abuser.

The actual instigation of breaking up, if this is an abusive romantic partner, might well not be a pleasant conversation. However, maintain your composure as much as possible and reinforce the notion that you are ending the relationship and moving on and that they need to respect this.

Different from more healthy breakups, you can choose to do this over text or call if you think this will put you in a safer position.

You do not need to justify your decision nor do you owe them any explanation.

They might try and fight, beg, or intimidate you into staying, but try to stay clear-headed and return to points 1 and 2 in reminding yourself why you are leaving in the first place.

Then, cut contact.

Delete and block numbers, block social media accounts, and tell your family and friends not to relay messages or answer calls.

This might be your first breakup. You have to commit to letting go. Else you will be stuck in the repeat cycle of a trauma bond.

We often decide to leave and go back, and find the person much unchanged despite their promises. So when you decide you are going to leave for good, I need you to tell me you are going to stick to that decision.

Eventual Healing: If you have successfully left an emotionally abusive relationship and the chances of you going back are low, you need to be incredibly proud of yourself.

You are likely in a raw and tender position.

There will be good days when you feel confident in your decision to leave and begin to feel yourself healing and growing. There will also be days when you miss your abuser; where you are tempted to reach out, maybe just to see how they are doing, or otherwise begin to regret ever having let them go.

As cliché as it sounds, it is critical that you are gentle with your feelings throughout and take some time to gather yourself. If it means time off work or an extended holiday, do it. Take the time you need to focus on yourself and make recalibration a priority.

You might be feeling a great deal of blame. As emotionally abusive relationships take such a toll on our self-esteem, you might be feeling regretful about leaving, or guilty. Maybe you feel like you deserved all that you went through.

Perhaps big karmic questions are running through your head and you are pondering why bad things happen to good people and what you did to deserve what you experienced.

However, you are likely carrying a fair deal of trauma and other emotions that come in the wake of an abusive relationship. Dealing with these will be explored more in the subsequent chapters, but for now, remind yourself that you are not responsible for the lives of others, and try and continue to reflect on the reasons why you left the relationship.

What to Do if the Abuser Tries to Re-Enter Your Life?

You have probably seen memes or posts about individuals going above and beyond to get beyond a social media block.

"Please unblock me," attached to $10 on PayPal.

"I want you back," with $100 on Cash App.

"I still need you," littering your spam request folder from newly made fake accounts.

An abusive partner who enjoys controlling might go above and beyond to try and reclaim you once you have left. This can be hurtful and incredibly damaging if you have consciously made the effort to create distance in your life, and is difficult to navigate.

However, block and report the accounts. Ignore the messages. Change your phone number. Remake your accounts.

If you feel like the attention is becoming too heavy and unwarranted and begins bordering on harassment, look into restraining orders to try and enforce the necessary distance between you and the individual in question.

The physical act of leaving is daunting, but this chapter should have provided you with the tools to build up an exit strategy and leave your abuser. Whether or not you are working up to this stage or have already left, I hope you can find some pride in even considering the notion of a life free from your abuser, as daunting as it might seem.

In the next chapter, we will begin working on life after an emotionally abusive relationship and healing strategies for emotional wounds and trauma.

Strengthening Our Collective Voice

Often, the aftermath of emotional abuse and the journey toward recovery can seem like an isolating path, filled with moments of self-doubt and a sense of being misunderstood. And yet, it is a path trodden by many – more than most of us realize.

This book has been a platform for you, me, and many others who have faced similar adversities, providing insights and strategies to cope with, and eventually overcome, the emotional trauma that has shaped our lives. It has opened up a dialogue – not just between you and me, the author, but between all of us who share this common journey.

Now, I extend an invitation to you, to become an active part of this shared narrative, not just as a reader but as a guiding light for others. And worry not, it does not ask much of your time or effort, just a few moments of honesty.

By leaving a review of this book on Amazon, you are showing fellow readers that they are not alone, that their struggles and challenges are understood, and most importantly, that there is a path toward healing. Your words can reaffirm that they are part of a larger community, striving towards recovery and healing, just like you.

Scan to leave a review

Share with them how this book has resonated with your experiences, or what insights it offered that they might also find within these pages. In doing so, you not only validate their journey but also point them in the direction of a resource that can guide them toward their own healing.

Each shared experience, each honest review, strengthens our collective voice, amplifying the message of resilience and recovery to those who need it most.

Thank you for your participation in this ripple effect of positive change. Together, we can redefine our narrative of emotional abuse and trauma, making a profound difference in our collective healing journey.

Chapter 5:
Healing Emotional Wounds and Trauma

You have left!

(Hopefully).

Congratulations.

As much as I would like to tell you that the hard work is over and the job is done, that would be a mistruth.

Perhaps naively, I was amongst those who believed that once I had left my relationship, I could move on swiftly and easily. I had toiled and battled with myself when deciding to leave. Having enacted it, surely, I could now rest easy.

Unfortunately, emotionally abusive relationships leave deep wounds, some of which take years to treat, and many of which leave lifelong scars.

But scars do not have to be bad things.

I look down at my light rippled scars and I am reminded of my strength and my resilience. Tiger stripes, if you will.

You will leave with stripes showing your courage, some of which you will carry for life.

Getting open wounds to the stage of scarring does however also take some work and active effort. Likely, you are not the same person you were when you entered into the relationship you have just left (unless this relates to a family member or parent).

Emotionally abusive relationships take a great toll on our self-worth. It often goes beyond superficial impressions of self-esteem and confidence to deep-rooted trauma.

What Is Trauma?

Deeply distressing psychological or emotional experiences can lead to trauma. Trauma does not have to be physical; emotional abuse can leave impactful trauma on how the brain functions and processes information, leading to a dysregulation in nervous system activity.

This can often lead to many of the below impacts, as well as a heightened sense of "fight or flight" when it comes to sensitivity in experiencing the world around us.

Impact of Emotionally Abusive Relationships

The impact that emotionally abusive relationships have upon victims can generally be categorized into long and short-term effects, which I have compiled below:

Short-Term Effects:

- Guilt
- Anxiety
- Shame
- Brain fog
- Mood swings

- Sadness and crying
- Trembling and shaking
- Insomnia
- Feeling lightheaded and faint
- Rapid breathing
- Changes in appetite

Long-Term Effects:

- **Loss of Identity:** Many victims of abuse leave the relationships feeling like they do not know themselves. Gaslighting and manipulation can erode a person's sense of individuality and faith in their hobbies and values, often leaving them feeling at odds with themselves.
- **Impacted Self-Esteem:** Alongside a sense of self, the esteem and confidence of victims of abuse are often greatly impacted (explored more in the following chapter).
- **Depression:** Victims of abuse can often go through depressive periods or begin experiencing diagnosable depression as a consequential mental health condition following emotional abuse.
- **Anxiety:** Many victims of abuse will also begin to extend beyond just feeling anxious and stressed to falling into the diagnosable category of having anxiety; whether social anxiety or generalized anxiety, or one of the many other sub-categories.

- **Substance Abuse:** Sufferers of emotional abuse may be more likely to turn to substance abuse or addiction to soothe themselves in heightened periods of stress.
- **Chronic Conditions Due to Prolonged Periods of Stress:** Extended periods of stress have been linked to chronic conditions such as chronic fatigue and irritable bowel syndrome (IBS).
- **Post-Traumatic Stress Disorder (PTSD):** A mental health issue developed after experiencing a traumatic event, including emotional abuse. This can lead to a combination of the above symptoms as well as experiencing flashbacks, having nightmares, and feeling physically frightened on a day-to-day basis.
- **Post-Betrayal Syndrome:** Issues associated with having been betrayed leading to an inability or difficulties in trusting others.

Inability to Trust Others

One of the most weary outcomes of an emotionally abusive relationship is the impact it has on our ability to trust other people.

Not just new romantic partners if you found yourself the victim of your partner or spouse, but also in areas of betrayal in friendship and in parent relationships.

Naively, I at least went into the world thinking people wished me well and meant well. I had good intentions and wanted the best for my friends and my partner, so I could not fathom why someone else would not want the same.

It did not even cross my mind that someone could so easily, so willingly, hurt another person before I experienced it firsthand. And being burned means you are less likely to play with fire in the future.

But unfortunately, not all fire is bad. In being burned by some relationships, those who have left may find themselves unable to trust any newcomers. They are skeptical about everyone's intentions; whether a colleague, a friend of a friend, or a potential flame. Where once lay a world of possibilities in terms of new friends and new flings lies now only danger.

As they say, once bitten, twice shy.

So the victims of abuse wrap themselves away in bubble wrap to avoid letting themselves get hurt another time. Or, as we have seen, they jump head first into new relationships before having done any healing or having worked on their self-esteem, in which they often fall victim to abusers yet again. Thus, the cycle repeats (but we will get on to that).

For the most part, you have to acknowledge where your trust has been broken. Perhaps you no longer trust your intuition or your judgment of character. That is okay – not all of us can guess someone's intentions correctly directly after meeting them.

However, trust is something that will play a part in your healing. Whilst difficult, learning to trust again is key to rebuilding relationships and forming a life after abuse. Although difficult, this also means sometimes giving people the benefit of the doubt.

I used to say, "You can have my trust until you break it."

Now I say, "You have to earn my trust."

The second statement is crucial as it means that in the time since the end of my emotionally abusive relationship, I have made myself vulnerable and allowed new people into my life – as much as it has scared me. This also took time. Five years of being single, to be precise.

But gradually, as my confidence grew, I took a deep breath and accepted that not everyone in the world has bad intentions.

However, if I was to invite new people into my life, I would have to approach them not with suspicion and mistrust, but with more caution.

It is a double-edged sword as whilst you want to make new friends and new partners, you have to outgrow your naivete in thinking everyone means you well and try and realistically assess and determine who is genuine and kind, and who is not.

At the same time, you cannot cut yourself off from everyone completely nor make them run rat races to prove you can trust them. Trust is just built gradually and consistently, through showing up for people, demonstrating your reliability and sincerity, and showing the goodness of your heart. You will find that you have to perform these actions and you will receive the same in return from the authentic and sincere individuals out there in the world.

Think of it for yourself – if you are willing to give the love and consistency you know you want to provide someone, you can be sure that there is someone out there willing to give you the same in return.

Inability to Trust Yourself

Generally, a consequence of being emotionally abused is not only the inability to trust others but an inability to trust your own intuition.

You are likely questioning whether or not you are a good judge of character. Asking yourself how you were so easily fooled. Wondering whether or not you can trust your own mind – especially if you were a victim of gaslighting and emotional manipulation.

Self-doubt and niggling worries that you cannot trust your own decision-making is a natural consequence of having been mistreated and having had your sense of reality warped.

Freshly out of an emotionally abusive relationship will likely mean you are still in the early stages of feeling vulnerable and doubtful about how you approach and assess others.

However, the ability to trust your own mind also comes with time and with rebuilding your self-esteem – which we will explore in the next chapter.

Impact on Social Life and Other Relationships

As covered above, you have likely lost a great deal of your capacity toward trusting other people. This will take time and effort to rebuild.

Equally, whilst you hopefully have reached out to old friends and family and rekindled relationships you may be cut off during your abusive relationship, there may be some people who do not want to re-enter your life. This is something you have to come to accept.

If you abandon friends and loved ones for a partner who turns out to be abusive, you can hope that they come back – but you must equally understand that relationships go two ways.

If you completely abandoned close friends during a relationship with an emotionally abusive partner, they might not be so willing to forgive and forget.

Whilst you might have come out the other side of an emotionally abusive relationship and began to heal, and now want to equally work on healing relationships you might have lost during that period, you also have to accept when your actions have hurt people.

Some might be unwilling to rekindle a friendship where they feel like they have been ignored or cast off in favor of their abuser.

However, friends come and go.

If you feel like your social circle is lacking after having left an emotionally abusive relationship and for whatever reason, you cannot reach back out to or reconnect with those people, do not be disheartened.

There are many other people in the world whom you have yet to meet, who will provide you with new friendships and new connections.

The key is taking on the trust that you gradually build and putting yourself back out there to find these people and rebuild your support network and social life.

Healing Strategies

As I have stressed, healing takes time and patience.

However, the first step toward healing is educating yourself and being honest with the situation you are in – which through taking the time to read through this book, you have already taken.

I have compiled a few strategies to assist in your healing journey that I personally found to be incredibly useful. These can be done in your own time – particularly for the first, this probably is not something you are considering if you are still in an active relationship with your abuser.

Having a wider view of these healing strategies in the back of your mind will help you to create a sense of where to direct your energy and where to focus when considering how to heal.

Forgiveness: As mentioned above, wounds left untreated can be left to fester.

Forgiveness may be a concept so far beyond where you are at in the current moment, but it is something to consider – maybe not now, but for the future.

Holding on to emotional anger and resentment and being unable to let it go can cause you to become stuck in a cycle of continually remembering old memories or being unable to let go of the past.

Forgiveness does not mean you are justifying or condoning your abuser's behavior. It does not mean that you want them back in your life. Abusers never "deserve" our forgiveness.

Forgiveness does not make you weak. Forgiveness is instead taking action and empowering yourself to let go of something that happened and someone who hurt you. Forgiveness is never a weakness; it takes a tremendous amount of courage and strength.

In forgiving, you move toward emotional freedom. You grow to recognize that people hurt us for their own reasons and that we are not responsible for these actions taking place, but we also no longer hold the actions against that person.

Forgiving has surprising benefits, such as:

- Releasing negative energy and stress you are harboring
- Using your experience to realize new aspects of your own character
- Empowering yourself
- Relinquishing any control your abuser still has over you

All of the above contribute to improved mental well-being and are conducive to rebuilding your sense of self-esteem.

You do not by any means have to reach out and tell your abuser that you forgive them. By no means do you have to text someone whom you have not spoken to in four years and say, "Hey, I forgive you! All the best."

When, and if, the time comes that you choose to forgive, you can keep this to yourself – forgiveness does not need to be vocalized. It comes purely from your heart and from within and needs only happen when you consider yourself ready.

Support Groups: Beyond rekindling old friendships and forging new ones, you will likely benefit from speaking to others who have been through similar experiences.

Support groups both online and in your area can help you to open up and share with people who understand your feelings.

Speaking to a friend or family member about your abuse can be helpful, however, unless someone has been through the same experience, they can often lack the right things to say or helpful suggestions. Not that this should be avoided in any case; they can still offer us a great deal of empathy and support.

However, reading about how you are not alone as a victim of abuse and learning about how other people have flourished in life after abuse can be immensely empowering, so do reach out and seek appropriate support from groups or communities if possible.

Therapy: Additionally, the guide of a licensed medical professional is also worth incorporating if feasible for your situation.

Therapists and counselors can help create healing programs and can lead you to uncover any deep-seated emotions, then help you to work through these.

Practical Guidance and Methods for Managing Post-Traumatic Stress

The below methods might be useful if you are trying to learn new ways in which to approach anxiety (if this is a symptom you are experiencing in life after abuse) and can help you to learn how to better regulate your emotions.

Whilst they might seem useless and unhelpful at first, these methods and techniques help to decrease anxiety and soothe the mind when frequently incorporated.

The "Window of Tolerance" (WOT): A term generally applied to knowing your limits in trying to balance your emotions and heal after a traumatic event.

Whilst within the limits of your WOT, you can generally manage everyday life stressors. The WOT for individuals experiencing PTSD symptoms or those who have been through an emotionally abusive relationship tends to be far lower, so being aware of what your comfortable limits are and keeping an eye out for trigger signs that you are pushing yourself too far (i.e. overtiredness, feeling agitated, feeling on the brink of a nervous breakdown) helps to know when you push and when to fall back so you avoid overwhelming yourself.

Learn Meditation and Breathwork Methods: These can help calm your nervous system and allow you to employ a greater sense of ease when you do begin to feel overwhelmed.

Approaching any form of mindfulness is made easier when you are more in control of your emotions. Paying attention to your breath can help calm your thoughts in most situations. It is also great to implement before you sit down and start trying to reflect on areas in which your self-worth needs improvement.

Something as simple as an inhale for 3 seconds, holding breath for 2, exhale for 4 seconds is perfect. Try and do this for a few minutes before engaging in self-reflection or do use it when you feel the anxious thoughts start to bubble.

Meditation can also be performed using free apps or podcasts, or by simply turning on a timer and trying to calm your thought space for a limited period.

It was also something I found incredibly challenging, to begin with. With my eyes closed, my head would fill with little inner voices critiquing me or things I had to tick off my to-do list the next day.

However, four years into meditating has helped me more than anything in learning how to quieten and control my mind. I am much more able to put a stop to negative thoughts before they spiral or to use meditation to better understand why I am feeling a certain way. Additionally, it is done wonders for my insomnia in being more able to turn off my thoughts and settle down.

Regulate Your Anxiety Using the 5-4-3-2-1 Method: A common emotional regulation method, this helps to divert your attention from a sudden overwhelming flood of emotions and helps you to calm yourself.

Shift your attention to your surroundings and try and find five things you can see (window, dog, table, orange, pencil), four things you can hear (bird, radio, fan, drilling), three things you could feel (velvet, fur, glass), two things you can smell (laundry, cinnamon), and one thing you can taste (a little harder but maybe a lingering aftertaste of coffee!)

Try and Shift Your Perspective to Happy Memories: I know – a lot easier said than done. However, if you find your mind spiraling into thoughts of self-doubt or anxiety, or you find yourself repeating a memory of your abusive relationship, try and bring something positive to the forefront of your mind and replace the negative thought.

I am not in any way saying that you should shut down negative thoughts or run and hide from them. There will come a time when you have to sit with and address every emotion but learn that your emotions do not control you or your response. Hiding from emotions only leads them to fester and grow until they begin to control us.

However, should you feel your mental state start to decline because of a temporary negative thought, for example, a memory of your abuser telling you that you are not good enough, think of something else. Displace the negative thought temporarily.

Think of a happy childhood memory, a beautiful sunset you saw, a pet if you have one. Even if only for a few seconds, focusing on a positive memory or feeling and stilling your breath can do wonders to regulate your mind.

This chapter covered the effects of emotionally abusive relationships; how much abusers can shake our worlds and leave us reeling both in the short-term and even years after the relationship.

If you are still in the midst of an emotionally abusive relationship, I hope you are more aware and educated about the toll that being manipulated and torn down can have on your emotional well-being.

Additionally, I hope that you are beginning to consider and put into practice self-care strategies to help yourself heal and techniques to care for your mind and your emotions.

In the next chapter, we will continue exploring techniques to rebuild your self-esteem and confidence.

Chapter 6:
Rebuilding Self-Esteem

Whilst you toil way at rebuilding your social life and other relationships, there is someone else you need to think about after coming out the other side of an emotionally abusive relationship.

Yes, you guessed it.

Yourself.

The person who takes the hardest hit coming out of an emotionally abusive relationship will always be the victim. Of course, family members and friends suffer the short-term loss of that person's presence. They generally do not however suffer the emotional burden and subsequent impact on self-esteem that many abusive relationships leave victims with.

Whilst the physical act of putting an end to an abusive relationship and leaving that person is often emotionally exhausting, you would not be the only person to come out the other side and feel like a stranger in your own body.

As many of the abuse tactics we have covered have demonstrated, abusers use their knowledge of us and our weaknesses and exploit it to their own advantage.

You think you can trust someone. You confide in them. You tell them you are a little bit insecure about your nose. It is probably your least favorite feature.

You leave that relationship feeling like you can only leave the house wearing a balaclava, you are so conscious of your nose. It is all you can see when you look in the mirror.

It does not just have to be physical attributes either. Emotionally manipulative people will whittle away at our insecurities regarding our intellect, our accent, our heritage, our humor. You name it – if it is a sore spot, it will be all the more tender once you have left that relationship.

I for one had done plenty of self-healing and confidence rebuilding before entering into the relationship I had with my ex.

However, much of that work was undone, and I started to notice old behaviors regarding body dysmorphia creep into my daily life after nearly a year of small comments and sly remarks regarding my size and shape.

On top of that, the general final months of our relationship had culminated in me getting pneumonia and losing two stone. I would like to think that the average young person is not so susceptible to pneumonia, but also cannot pin this down on an ex. However, the stress of trying to hold together a relationship that was crippling me, knowing full well my partner was being unfaithful, being gaslit and belittled all caused me and my body immense stress.

I did not relapse into my eating disorder, but I ended that relationship further back on the path to healing than I had started.

Not only that – I was suddenly far more conscious of other aspects of myself beyond my physical appearance. I was, after all, cold and callous. Unemotional and uncaring. Weird.

My demeanor had driven a man to cheat. Or at least, so I had been told. And as victims of abusive relationships generally take these statements to heart and lack the clarity or resilience to ward off such aggravating claims, his comments stayed with me for years. A little voice quoting these comments rose not only when I considered putting myself forward to new friends, new partners, and new situations, but also followed me around when I got home to my quiet little apartment and got into my bed.

That is the sad thing about emotionally abusive relationships. We can leave the instigator, but the wounds we still have to carry.

So the question is, how do we turn those wounds into scars? How do we heal the damage an abuser has done to us and rebuild our self-esteem, so that we can present ourselves with the confidence and poise we are more than deserving of?

Well firstly, and most importantly, you have to realize that it takes time. The depth of your wounds can vary. Being in a relationship with an abuser can leave damage so deep it seems irreparable. An emotionally abusive parent, for example, can leave you feeling like all you know is degradation and criticism. It is all you have ever known, since birth.

But even in a short stint with an emotionally abusive partner or friend can you still end up with surprising amounts of damage which take years to heal. It sounds daunting, I know. But you need patience when approaching healing and rebuilding your self-esteem.

As much as I would like to tell you that getting out is the hard part, you are probably starting to realize quite the toll emotionally abusive relationships can take on us having read the previous chapter.

The good news is that all things can be rebuilt. In many cases, it is not even a case of rebuilding, but of growing. You will begin to see your confidence creep back in, you will learn new things about yourself, and you will emerge as a different person from who you were before you entered into this past relationship.

That is not a bad thing.

It is difficult to grasp the idea that you will come out of this experience as a better person. Especially if you are currently in the beginning stages of your journey, you might feel despairing and hopeless. You just want to have the confidence you had when you went on your first date with your abuser. You want that person's shine back.

But through practicing the elements of forgiveness covered in the previous chapter, you will gradually grow to let go of not only your abuser but whatever ideal you hold of yourself that you wistfully look back upon.

Maybe you also hold on to some element of guilt for letting that person, that younger version of yourself, get so trodden up by one person. Yet that guilt you might be feeling for not having protected yourself better is something we will also address.

And I promise you, no one has a magical-looking glass. No one can see into the future, nor can we always tell when someone has good intentions from when someone really has only their own interests at heart.

The prospect of ever going on another date again might seem lifetimes away. If that is the case, do not rush yourself. In this chapter, we will work together on learning what it takes to rebuild your self-esteem and pick your confidence back up after an emotionally abusive relationship.

Maybe you will learn about more ways in which this relationship impacted your self-worth which you have not yet thought to consider. Maybe you will find the techniques and strategies I have personally found to be useful in my own healing journey beneficial to your own.

Whatever the case, rebuilding takes time. If that means entering a cocoon-like state for a while whilst you withdraw and heal, that is more than acceptable. Use the WOT approach we covered in the previous chapter to try and understand your limits better and know when to push in rebuilding self-esteem, and when to take a step back and focus on self-care.

Rebuilding Self-Worth

Before we get knee-deep into how to rebuild your self-esteem, let us make sure we are on the same page when it comes to what self-worth actually is.

Self-worth is defined as how you love, respect, and value yourself. This often also impacts the degree to which you feel worthy of outside love and respect.

Self-esteem is a more limited and specific feeling of confidence in yourself and your abilities. This is often impacted by external factors.

The above can be easily mixed up, but are not to be confused. You can have high self-esteem but low self-worth. A cliché example, but take an influencer for example. They have adoring online fans and spend hours perfecting their appearance. They strut into events with confidence and style, and at times experience an incredibly high level of self-esteem at points and feel on top of the world. Yet they might still lack self-worth and find themselves moving the extra mile to gain validation, to better benefit their short-term self-esteem.

Chances are, after a toxic relationship where you have fallen victim to emotional abuse, you are lacking in self-worth, self-esteem, and self-confidence.

Where Do You Start?

Building up self-esteem is a marathon, not a race. I personally have found the following stages to be incredibly useful when it comes to pinpointing my insecurities and areas in which I need or needed to improve. I was able to tackle those areas in a way that did not overwhelm me but allowed me to calm my emotions and direct all that effort I was putting into feeling negatively about myself, in a constructive way.

1. Awareness

It is difficult to rebuild and heal wounds that you are not aware of. So, the first step is sitting down and reflecting on how you are truly feeling, and how you think your relationship (or other traumatic experiences) has impacted your self-worth.

It is often difficult to reflect objectively. It is ten times harder when you are in a state of heightened emotions.

Using mindfulness to calm your emotions and begin to delve deeper into your thinking patterns often helps open doorways to undercurrent trauma or wounds we did not know existed, or were previously blind to.

Mindfulness means focusing your awareness on the present moment and calmly accepting whatever emotions you are feeling. It is often not easily achieved on your own. The below tools will help identify areas where you might need to focus a little extra on improving your self-esteem and self-worth.

Breathwork: Approaching any form of mindfulness is made easier when you are more in control of your emotions. We covered some key strategies that you can use to ease your sense of mind and divert anxious thoughts in the previous chapter which may be useful to reflect upon.

Incorporate breathwork into your daily routine and use it when you need to calm your thoughts and start digging deep into your self-awareness.

Meditation: The thought of having to meditate can seem exhausting for newbies, but believe me, I was once in your position too. The positive effects of meditation on mental health are however too good not to be conscious of. Regularly meditating not only helps to alleviate depression and anxiety but has been also linked to overall health and wellness such as lower risks of heart disease and other illnesses.

This is not to say that being open to the idea of medication is a bad idea. Medications in conjunction with meditation and therapy can often be hugely beneficial in getting you far further in your journey to self-discovery than doing it completely solo.

Starting to regularly meditate can be daunting, but consider trialing a free app (of which there are many). If using apps is not your thing, you can experiment with guided meditations on streaming platforms or try setting a timer and sitting down in a calm and safe environment. With your eyes closed, try to clear your mind. This might mean using the above and focusing on your breathing, at least for the initial stages of learning to meditate. Whilst you might find that your mind becomes flooded with thoughts of things you have to do tomorrow and niggling worries of self-doubt, the aim is to quieten these voices and deflect them. In time, you will grow to have better control over your thoughts and be able to put an end to negative thoughts before they begin to spiral.

Additionally, meditation can lead your mind to new places of unexplored trauma and bring you great enlightenment. You will be surprised to find what you uncover once you start opening your mind.

2. Journaling

Finally, keeping a written track of how you are feeling and what you think has triggered these thoughts can be helpful.

Not everyone enjoys writing down nor has the time, but looking back and being able to visualize your progress is often one of the biggest motivators in healing and self-discovery.

Consider journaling the following:

- Where you see yourself next month/year/5 years
- What you like about yourself
- What you dislike about yourself
- What about you that you think has changed after your relationship
- Any guilt or shame you feel, and any root causes you can identify
- Triggering situations or emotions that leave you feeling more overwhelmed than normal
- Strategies and behaviors that help you
- Potential techniques you have yet to try out
- What do you envision yourself being like in an ideal world
- Ways in which you can work toward becoming more like your ideal

3. Goal Setting

On top of answering the above questions in your journal, a great way to build self-esteem and self-worth is to achieve goals.

I do not mean going out and climbing Mount Everest (although you are welcome to put that on you are bucket list, and if you do make it to the top, I will be in absolute awe as will you of your own resilience).

The goals can be minor and do not have to be in any way related to your relationship history or your current characteristics.

For example:

- Reading one book per month
- Finishing a jigsaw puzzle
- Not going on your phone for a whole day
- Doing something that scares you

If you feel like you are suffering from some of the symptoms of trauma and PTSD such as depression or anxiety, consider how you might actively tackle these concerns even on a daily or weekly scale. This might include facing social anxiety concerns or performing small household chores that have others become more difficult owing to depression.

For example:

- Texting a friend whom you have not spoken to in a while
- Attending a concert
- Doing the laundry

- Watering your houseplants

The simple act of setting a goal and ticking the box can provide a huge sense of accomplishment, even if it is minor. Being able to reflect on these goals you have set and completed will gradually build up to provide you with a developed can-do attitude; particularly if you are feeling listless and lacking in energy.

4. Physical Health

You might not love the gym or running. You might also enjoy indulging in sugar and treats and have found that in the time since ending your relationship, you have indulged in things that provide you with a short-term high more than normal.

Perhaps you have had more lazy days binge-watching your favorite shows. Maybe you have started (or resumed) smoking or vaping. Maybe you have been drinking alcohol a bit more than normal.

It is perfectly normal to incorporate more of these soothing behaviors immediately after a traumatic event or in the initial healing stages. However, continuing to involve behaviors that are detrimental to your health will only degrade your self-worth further.

As I want deeply to avoid the cliché of you sitting around in your pajamas and eating ice cream to absolve your thoughts, packing on pounds, and feeling bad about your body, I can provide an alternate example.

After I left my own emotionally abusive relationship, I went in the opposite direction to many. I threw myself headfirst into exercising. It alleviated my anxiety and was almost the only time when my brain was not consumed by other thoughts.

Headphones in, music jacked up to full volume, I could not hear myself think – let alone think about my memories with my abuser or how I felt about myself now.

Working out also made me feel good. Having lost a lot of my purpose and identity, I started to focus a huge portion of my life on working out, eating in a way that was restrictive but would fuel my body, and organizing my lifestyle to prioritize my capacity to work out.

As I have mentioned, having suffered from a restrictive eating disorder throughout my teens, this was not the most healthy coping approach.

Additionally, I quickly found myself rejecting social invitations from my friends because it involved staying up too late (when I wanted to be fresh and invigorated for the day head), or saying no to dinners or nights out as alcohol and restaurant food did not align with my vision and current purpose.

Self-esteem and self-worth can be hugely impacted by physical health. This does not mean hitting the gym six days a week and living off protein shakes, nor does it mean going to spin classes at 6 AM every morning.

Move in ways that feel good for you. Yoga, hiking, salsa classes. There are so many ways in which you can get active without conforming to the more normative idea of going to the gym or going for a run.

Exercise also has huge benefits for your self-esteem. Dopamine rush aside, feeling good about yourself, and having scheduled activities to participate in help to build a routine.

Particularly if you are struggling to find motivation or purpose after losing a large portion of yourself in an emotionally abusive relationship, activities like a Thursday night dance class, a Sunday yoga session, or even a morning walk with your dog give you opportunities to meet people and structure your weeks.

However, as mentioned above, be cautious (for those with a more addictive personality amongst you), to incorporate these in moderation.

For many of the reasons listed in earlier chapters, the nature of many people who fall into relationships with abusers makes them more susceptible to this addictive behavior.

Whilst we will cover how to avoid falling into another emotionally abusive relationship, you also want to break the cycle of abuse (or at least avoid it) replacing your addiction and trauma bond to your abuser with an addiction to a substance or a behavior.

As the saying goes, "Everything in moderation."

5. Social Life

Perhaps you are aware and conscious of the fact that your social life has been impacted in the aftermath of an emotionally abusive relationship, or if you just want to make more friends, both will do wonders for building your self-esteem and self-worth.

Through meeting new people (and in this case, people who respect us), it is key that you take away some of these learnings and apply them to how you view individuals in the future to avoid relapsing into toxic relationships). You will learn more about the world and yourself.

Putting yourself out there is a daunting prospect, but try where possible (using your frame of reference of your WOT) to push yourself to attend events and socialize.

I know I am not one to talk. I spent months after my relationship ended hibernating at home, rescinding invitations for dinner or simply my friends offering to come and visit me to stew in my own company. I felt safer that way.

However, a time will come when you will benefit more from putting yourself out there and enjoying the company of others.

For me, it is always a case of being extremely anxiety-inducing and "I would rather stay at home." I however muster up the courage to go, and return home elated and filled with positive energy, having made new memories, met new people, and learned new things.

On top of reaching out to old friends, consider where you might meet new people. Speed-dating might not be on the cards yet, but trying out new activities such as yoga or dance as mentioned above can open doorways for you to form new connections.

Whilst I never condone using the validation of other people to boost your self-worth, you will likely find that in time, you will form new friendships. These people will contribute to your self-esteem and self-worth. Surprisingly, not everyone means you harm nor will weaponize your insecurities against you. I have made friends whom I have confided in, who have for decades remained sensitive to my sensitivities and supported me endlessly. There are good people out there; it sometimes just takes a couple of goes (maybe kissing a couple of toads) to find them.

Whilst the wounds of an emotionally abusive relationship might still be fresh, there are still many other people out there who are eager to meet you, who will accompany you on adventures, and who will bring out the best in you.

Challenging Negative Thoughts

Our sense of self and self-esteem often becomes so impacted due to comments and behaviors instigated by abusers, and then the internal thoughts we carry with us even after terminating the relationship.

Therefore, building up methods to challenge these negative thoughts is key. Although always easier said than done, consider some of the following methods when you start to feel like there is a little voice in your head telling you that you are not good enough, that you are in some way aesthetically displeasing, and that you are not intelligent enough.

Distractions: Firstly, if you feel your thoughts spiraling and you start sinking into a whirlwind of self-doubt, try to intervene early. This takes self-discipline and control which both take time to cultivate as well.

However, look out for trigger signs when your mood or thoughts do begin to spiral and try to stop them in their tracks.

We covered some anxiety easing methods in the previous chapter which will be of use. Additionally, you can try going for a walk, when possible (my favorite tool), doing a short meditation practice, or organizing your sock drawer.

The aim of this is to put a stop to negative self-talk before it is allowed to spiral. Gradually, by deflecting your attention elsewhere, your tendency to start ruminating on your own shortcomings or your past relationship will happen less and less.

Thought Replacement: Additionally, aside from physical distractions, you can also begin to incorporate cognitive restructuring into your thought processes.

This is a difficult skill to master at first. Essentially, it is a bit like swapping an apple for an orange.

Say you begin to start dwelling on your body image, or your lack of ability to complete a project. You feel those doubts start to wrap around you and compel you to not leave the house today, or to tell your manager that you simply cannot do it.

To replace these negative thoughts, have a set of internal questions in mind that you pose to yourself when you start to feel self-doubt overwhelming you. Your questions might differ, but try and base them on the following:

- Is this thought realistic?
- Why am I thinking this? Is there anything in my past that has triggered these emotions?
- What will I gain by continuing to think about this topic?
- Am I catastrophizing? (Thinking the absolute worst scenario, which in many cases is quite unlikely to come about).

Then, where possible, try to intervene and instead replace negative thoughts with positive ones. You do not need to overdo it with unrealistic and overly positive statements. For example, if you are experiencing some anxiety over your body image, trying to adamantly think, "I adore every inch of my body" is less helpful than "I accept myself as I am and know I am an individual."

Or, if doubting your ability, avoid "I am going to succeed no matter what," and try to focus on something more neutral like "I will try my best and I will be proud of what I achieve, no matter what that looks like."

Managing and controlling your thoughts in this way is incredibly difficult to begin with, but gets easier (as all things do) with practice.

Self-Affirmations: Self-affirmations or positive affirmations are short statements that you can use to help refocus your thoughts and brighten your perspective on both yourself and your situation.

Back to the journaling ... boring for some of you, I know! Writing some of the below down (tailored to yourself and your own situation) will help you to then be able to reflect and focus as a form of distraction during tougher days. Write a few down in the notes app on your phone or a scrap piece of paper and repeat them in your head (or out loud, depending on where you are) to remind yourself of how worthy you are and how much you deserve.

- I am worthy of love and happiness.
- I embrace my uniqueness and celebrate who I am.
- I am beautiful inside and out.
- I have the power to create positive change in my life.
- I am resilient and capable of overcoming any challenge.
- I am deserving of success and abundance.
- I choose to see the good in myself and others.
- I am enough just as I am.
- I radiate confidence and attract positive experiences.
- I am proud of my accomplishments, big and small.
- I release negative self-judgment and embrace self-acceptance.
- I am surrounded by love and support from those who care about me.
- I am a work in progress, and I embrace the journey of self-growth.
- I forgive myself for past mistakes and allow myself to move forward.

- I am worthy of respect and kindness from others.
- I trust in my ability to make wise decisions for myself.
- I am strong, capable, and deserving of happiness.
- I am grateful for the unique gifts and talents I possess.
- I attract positive, uplifting people into my life.
- I am worthy of love and affection.
- I release comparisons and appreciate my own journey.
- I am allowed to set boundaries and prioritize my own well-being.
- I am a magnet for opportunities and abundance.
- I am worthy of self-care and taking time for myself.
- I embrace my imperfections and understand they make me unique.
- I choose to focus on my strengths and build upon them.
- I am surrounded by positivity and joy in every aspect of my life.
- I am proud of myself for how far I have come.
- I have the power to create the life I desire.
- I love and accept myself unconditionally.

Whilst I remain at times shy and reserved, I have come miles since the end of my relationship. I would not be the only one to tell you that, either.

"You are like a different person," my best friend told me. "The foundations are still the same. You are still … you. You have just become so much more confident in yourself."

It can be difficult to track changes in our self-worth and confidence from the inside. You might work tirelessly to incorporate these self-worth-building strategies but still find yourself exasperated on the days you end up slumped in negative thoughts and self-doubt.

The beauty is that those days will become less frequent. And the truth is that everyone experiences them.

Whilst the psychological impact of being in an emotionally abusive relationship does leave you feeling like you are starting ten steps back in terms of confidence, there is nothing to stop you from catching up.

As you begin to try new experiences, remind yourself of your worth and your ability, and push yourself outside of your comfort zone, you too will flourish.

In this chapter, we have covered tools and techniques you can implement to help work on what is likely an impaired sense of self-worth. You are not alone in this – I share your pain in having left a relationship with someone I adored, feeling like a tattered and shredded version of my former self.

Healing takes time. However, through practicing mindfulness and meditation and implementing self-care, you too can begin to rebuild your sense of self and realize how worthy you are.

In our final chapter, we will cover how to navigate future relationships, and how to construct boundaries that allow newcomers into your life whilst protecting the self-esteem you have worked so hard to repair.

Chapter 7:
Thriving Beyond Abuse - Life After Abusive Relationships

The sheer courage and will that get to the point of accepting that you are in an emotionally abusive relationship and choosing to leave is colossal. Those on the outside who have not experienced similar relationships will never truly understand the pain and suffering it costs us to leave behind those whom we love or loved, who have hurt us.

To love means also to let go – especially if that person is covered in thorns and leaves you bleeding.

Emotionally abusive relationships are also in themselves very lonely experiences. For many of us, we enter into them thinking that we have found a missing piece of ourselves. An anxious yearning to be loved and be wanted leaves us more inclined to gloss over how this person is hurting us. However, whether conscious of it or not, we often end up feeling lonelier in the relationship than previously.

Coming out of emotionally abusive relationships, romantic or not, people often go one of two ways; they close themselves off and keep everyone at arm's length to not be hurt again, or they fling themselves desperately into a relationship with the next person they see coming to try and fill the void.

I personally went for a blend of the two. For four or five years, I avoided dating. I studied. I traveled. I went to bed early and read books. I had nothing to add to conversations where my friends gossiped about dates they had been on, or compared boys they had matched with on apps.

I was absolutely terrified of falling into the same trap. Dating, which had previously been fun and engaging, seemed like a petrifying sport. I looked at every man and saw the reflection of my ex, and decided it was best to keep them all at arm's length.

Occasionally, someone would ask why I was not participating. Why did I not fancy meeting a friend or a friend who they argued would be "just my type." Why not just give the apps a go? Why was I not a little more forthcoming to strangers who approached us on nights out and try to twirl us around?

All of these I declined with a polite nod. Having recently moved cities, my ex had been a fleeting presence in the lives of my new friends. I had given no reasonings for our breakup apart from the trials and tribulations of long distance. They had met him in passing once or twice but had hardly spoken a word. Typically, I had been nothing but positive when talking about our relationship, albeit only in snippets. In their eyes, there had been nothing amiss; just the natural conclusion of a long-distance relationship. It was years later that I gradually started opening up and being honest about the things he had said to me and the dynamic I had endured.

At some point, I decided that it was time for me to resume dating. It was not an easy comeback for me. Whilst I had gone to therapy and read books, addressed my past trauma, and worked on healing, I was not completely ... healed.

It is very difficult to put an actual end goal for where you would consider yourself healed, as in healing, you grow. You never stop growing as self-discovery continues throughout your life, so it is an ongoing process and a journey as opposed to waking up one morning and deciding you are done healing.

My goal has never been to hold your hand and drag you along to the finishing line. Rather, I hope to share with you the tools that you can learn about and continue to implement throughout your own healing journey.

Whilst we have already covered the importance of redefining and discovering your self-worth, it is also important to address how you will approach and navigate relationships with other people.

Life continues after emotionally abusive relationships. Even if the prospect of inviting new people into your life seems now too daunting, there will come a point in the future when you are ready to start forming new connections and putting yourself out there.

Do not let others pressure you into doing so. Nor should you feel guilty and start pressuring yourself into dating or making new friends or trying new experiences if you do not feel ready (remember to keep your WOT in mind). But future relationships will come, and I want more than anything to make sure that this is not a pattern that you repeat.

To be able to maintain healthy relationships without sacrificing your sense of self or your feelings of self-worth, you need pretty good boundaries in play.

In an ideal world, people respect our boundaries and do not encroach on them. Someone knows that you do not like being hugged, so they do not hug you without your permission. Another person knows that you are uncomfortable talking about your family life, so they never push you or ask questions.

However, emotionally abusive individuals and narcissists do not tend to respect or value the boundaries of other people. Being in a relationship with such a person, who disrespects and ignores your boundaries, can leave you feeling like you do not know your own boundaries and they certainly do not matter.

The issue is that boundary setting is key to being able to invite other people into your life, to love them and to trust them, but also to protect yourself.

Generally, there are 6 subtypes of boundaries:

Physical Boundaries: These include your personal space, how comfortable you are with physical touch, and your personal needs when it comes to exercising and eating.

Examples:

"I do not enjoy hugs, let us shake hands instead."

"I need to take tonight off because I am really tired."

"I do not eat meat."

Emotional Boundaries: These revolve around setting boundaries for your emotional needs; how much you can support another person and their feelings, what you are comfortable sharing and what you want people to avoid asking about, and how you step away from scenarios where your emotional needs get compromised.

Examples:

"I do not want to talk about my childhood with you. That is not a topic I am comfortable sharing."

"I understand that you are having a really hard time with this but I do not think I am emotionally capable of supporting you right now."

"I am having a rough time right now. Are you free to talk through this with me?"

Time Boundaries: Your time is precious. We all have limited time, especially as we grow older, and need to protect how we spend it and with whom. This means setting limits as to how you spend your time in your personal and professional lives, and also prioritizing certain time-consuming actions over others so you do not end up feeling overstressed and overburdened.

Examples:

"I cannot come out this evening."

"I need to leave by 8 PM."

"I am happy to work on it for four hours."

Sexual Boundaries: Experimentation is great, but consent is more important. Knowing what you are comfortable doing in the bedroom and making sure your partner knows and respects these is incredibly important.

Sexual boundaries can include:

Discussing what you are and are not comfortable with

Requesting the use of contraception

Asking for consent

Intellectual Boundaries: We all have different values and opinions, and part of life is respecting the beliefs of others. You can discuss and debate and enjoy doing so, but you should never belittle others when they think differently from you, nor should you have your own ideas belittled.

Examples:

"Let us agree to disagree as we both think differently on this."

"I enjoy hearing how differently you think about this issue but I would appreciate if you respect that I was raised differently so do not think in the same way."

"I love hearing your opinions on this matter but can we save this conversation for another day?"

Material Boundaries: Finally, your personal property and finances also fall under boundary protection. Setting appropriate boundaries about how people interact with your personal possessions is also important and prevents you from feeling like people are taking advantage of your possessions or money.

Examples:

"I do not want you to use my car."

"I am not comfortable lending you money but I can try and help you fill some job applications."

"You can borrow my jeans but I need them back by Tuesday."

Setting Boundaries

Now you know about the different types of boundaries, how do you set them? How do you make sure you enforce clear rules and try your best to enforce consequences so that in the future, people will respect the boundaries you have placed – unlike your abuser?

Define Your Boundaries: To start, it is difficult to protect yourself and communicate your boundaries to other people if you do not know your boundaries yourself.

Often, we put the "chill person" up on a pedestal. Women get demonized for being controlling or "bossy," when in fact they are just on top of knowing what they need and protecting their peace. The same goes for men, although "bossy," might not be used in quite such a negative light. People latch on to the term "boundary" and start trying to use it to control what other people are doing as opposed to what they are comfortable with.

You can set a boundary for people in your life, but in doing so, you are not telling them what they can and cannot do. Only they can decide what they are allowed to do. You are simply expressing what you are comfortable with.

You might tell your partner that physical cheating or emotional cheating will lead to an immediate breakup. In saying this, you are not telling them that they cannot cheat. If they want to, they do as they please. What you are communicating is that infidelity is beyond your boundaries and that such actions will have consequences (such as ceasing the relationship).

Controlling your partner or your friends is not what we are aiming for. Everyone lives autonomously and part of life is interacting with people who see the world very differently from you and finding compromises and middle ground between those differing viewpoints.

To do so, you need to understand and be firm in what your boundaries are.

Self-reflection will help the most in this. If after exiting an emotionally abusive relationship, where your needs came second and your boundaries were never respected, you are not entirely sure what your boundaries are any more, consider sitting down and asking yourself the following questions:

- What level of physical interaction makes me uncomfortable?
- What topics am I not comfortable discussing?
- What areas of self-care (e.g. exercise, nutrition, sleep) do I need to prioritize to feel my best?
- What views or beliefs do I hold that I do not appreciate people belittling?

Communicate Your Boundaries: Once you have a clearer idea of your boundaries, you then need to communicate them to a partner or friend.

People are not mind readers. Even in healthy relationships, we can sometimes get upset when our partners or friends do something that we are not comfortable with. Yet, if they were not to know that this was beyond what you are comfortable with, it is difficult to justify getting upset (unless it is pretty common sense).

Sitting down on a first date with a long list of what you consider to be okay and not okay is not the right way forward. However, having check-ins with long-term partners and discussing what each of you is comfortable with is conducive to understanding both of your limits.

Equally, you might not be able to communicate a boundary unless the issue arises. For example, if you dislike physical touch, you are unlikely to announce this to everyone you meet straightaway. It might take someone trying to bearhug you, you communicating this boundary, and them then understanding your limits to set certain boundaries.

Enforce Your Boundaries by Saying "No" and Having Consequences: Here comes the tricky one ...

In emotionally abusive relationships, we often bend to someone else's will. There might have been points in the past where you spoke up and told your abuser that you were not comfortable with something, and they just laughed at you or ignored you. Over time, our loved ones ignoring or pushing our boundaries can leave us feeling disrespected and undervalued – which we remedy by then allowing others to traipse over our boundaries. The thought process in our heads tends to run a little like this: This person does not/did not respect me. If I was worthy of respect, they would not have done that. I do not really respect myself and I do not feel like other people will either.

This is a very sad but common outcome in the thinking of victims of emotional abusers. Maybe you did have the confidence to once upon a time pipe up and say no, but having just been laughed at in the process, you have learned to shut your mouth and people-please.

Learning to say "No" is one of the most challenging elements of boundary setting. It is critical to building future relationships and making sure that people respect you. It is hard, I know. You worry that people will think you are too strict and no fun. You worry that they will leave you because of these elements (and if you suffer from an anxious attachment style and crave affection and attention, being abandoned can seem like the scariest thing in the world).

Conversely to all those doubts about sticking up for yourself, people will respect you more if you say "No" to things that you are not comfortable with.

On top of that, you need to enforce some form of consequence for those that continuously push your boundaries.

In the same way that you need to reflect on your boundaries, you also need to have a set of limits and consequences for people who ignore them.

Ultimatums are one approach to consequences. They sound a little like "If you continue ignoring my boundaries when it comes to going through my phone and doing it once more, we will have to break up."

Ultimatums are difficult to enforce if you have a history of people-pleasing. Setting an ultimatum like the above and then not following through with it, but instead giving the person another chance, then another, just means you continue to lose respect for one another. They think you do not stick by your boundaries, and you think they do not respect you enough to listen to your limits.

Whilst there are definitely deal breakers and non-negotiable actions which require a termination of the relationship and ultimatum, it is often better to approach people disrespecting your boundaries with consequences.

For example, if someone repeatedly tries to bring up a topic you have expressed your discomfort in discussing, you walk away. If someone is repeatedly late to a meetup or a date, you cease waiting for them and just leave. If a colleague continues to talk over you or interrupt you despite you asking them not to, you raise it to HR.

None of the above have to end in conflict or aggression. Maintaining your boundaries requires using many of the anxiety regulation methods we have covered to stay calm and composed when interacting with that person, and then escalating the matter in a non-reactive way.

Remind Yourself That You Deserve Respect: In setting and maintaining relationships with people, you will likely run into doubt and wonder if you are overdoing it. You might at points be tempted to forego your boundaries and let people do as they please out of fear of upsetting them or driving them away.

When these feelings arise, try and return to the techniques and strategies covered in the previous chapter. Remind yourself that you are worthy. Self-confidence and knowing your boundaries feed off of one another; knowing your limits and boundaries helps you to feel more confident in yourself and your worth, and self-confidence makes enforcing those boundaries and shutting off those who ignore your needs easier.

As your life continues in the aftermath of an emotionally abusive relationship, these boundary-setting techniques will be critical in giving you the tools to then start trusting other people again.

Whilst initially trusting new people and their intentions is difficult, you will at least know that you can trust yourself to make the right decisions; uphold your boundaries, communicate them effectively to other people, and enforce consequences for when people disrespect you.

So even if you start pushing yourself to date or befriend new people and still feel uneasy about other people, you can trust and still feel uneasy about other people, you can trust yourself to make the right decisions and cut off newcomers who start showing similar behavior to the emotionally abusive individuals in your past.

In the future, you will encounter people who also exhibit emotionally abusive behaviors. I wish I could say otherwise, and I wish I could protect you from them. But the truth is that not everyone has a kind heart, and your ex, partner, friend, parent – whoever you have worked so hard to let go of – is not the only person who is capable of emotionally manipulating and gaslighting people to their own advantage.

However, you will now know what to look out for.

This is key as whilst helping you to break free from the grasp of one emotionally abusive individual and heal the wounds they have left you with, I want more than anything to break a future cycle of abuse. Individuals who are suspectable to abusers often never free themselves from this cycle.

They fall into future relationships with equally abusive individuals, having never worked on their self-worth, their ability to say "No," or to walk away.

As parents, they either exemplify this behavior to their children who grow up to mirror it and fall victim to abusive relationships, or they take on the role of the abuser when finally in a position of power.

That is not how I want your story to play out. You are in charge of your narrative and your ending. Well, to a degree. We cannot whisper to fate about the happily-ever-after we want, but we can learn how to distinguish emotionally abusive individuals and how to protect ourselves.

We all make mistakes in life. We fall for the wrong people and fail to see what is really happening.

My concluding aim is to provide you with the tools to be able to see when a new co-worker or a new person in your friend group falls into the category of an emotional manipulator. I want you to be able to tell when someone is love bombing you. I want you to be able to see through a parent-in-law weaponizing your insecurities or those of your partner against you.

I will avoid trying to dress up your trauma as a positive experience, but learning first-hand is often the best way to learn. Having gone through what you have and now working to educate yourself and protect yourself, you will be more equipped to be able to identify emotional abusers than those who have not experienced such abuse.

Whilst you might look back on your past and wish you had done things differently; you have likely learned a great deal about yourself and other people through experiencing what you have. The courage you have fostered in leaving and the resilience you have in wanting to rebuild yourself are both indicators of an incredibly strong-willed daring mind (even if it does not seem like it right now).

One day, I hope you will be able to look back to where you are today with kindness and tenderness; look back to where you once were and how alone you felt, but also have pride in how far you have come. The strength it takes to leave an emotionally abusive relationship, work through your trauma, and rebuild your self-esteem is immense. You will be able to take your resilience and strength of character onwards to other areas of life and use it to your advantage (or just write about your experience and help others – like me!)

A Call for Your Valued Thoughts

Dear Reader,

I sincerely hope that this book has provided you with the understanding and insights you were seeking. As you apply the strategies discussed and embark on your own journey toward healing, remember that there are others who are also searching for guidance and strategies for emotional abuse and trauma recovery.

By taking a few moments to leave an honest review of this book on Amazon, you help others to find this resource, which might be the lifeline they have been searching for.

Scan to leave a review

As an independent author, your feedback is incredibly important. It not only helps the success of this book but also assists in making sure that it reaches those who need it the most. I would be profoundly grateful if you could spare a moment to leave a review on Amazon, rest assured, every word will be read and cherished personally.

Your insights, whether they be commendations or critiques, are greatly appreciated. Thank you for taking the time to share your thoughts.

Warm regards,

Miriam Sutton

Conclusion

Congratulations on finishing "Emotional Abuse and Trauma Recovery."

Wherever you are in your journey through navigating a relationship with someone who is emotionally abusive, I hope you can leave feeling more informed and empowered.

Choosing to love someone who does us harm, even if that choice is beyond our control, if they come in the form of a parent, or if we are just so desperate to be loved, is a painful experience.

However, love does not need to always hurt. There will be people out there who value you, who treat you with respect, and who are sensitive to your sensitivities. They will never use your insecurities against you.

And whilst re-entering into relationships might seem like a far-off vision if you are still in an active relationship with an abuser, I hope that you have realized how worthy you are of a love that lifts you, and how that person cannot provide such affection.

For the time being, you will know that you must love yourself first and foremost. In doing so, you will know the importance of working to rebuild your confidence and self-esteem, how to manage your emotions, and how to move on in life with boundaries that protect everything you have worked for and everything you are.

For my final words; remember that healing is a journey, not a destination. The journey might seem long and tiresome at points, but you will continue to build upon that courage and resilience you have shown in finishing this book and be able to take on that hard-earned perseverance to other elements in your life.

You are already far stronger than you think.

About The Author

Miriam Sutton, widely recognized for her insightful prose, has devoted herself to the exploration of personal growth, resilience, and the transformative power of self-discovery. Drawing from a wellspring of personal experiences and years of introspective practice, she navigates the intricate path of emotional well-being with an empathetic and steady hand.

Her voyage into the world of personal development was ignited by a life-altering event that prompted her to turn inwards, re-evaluate her perspective, and seek out healing. This powerful self-reflective journey acted as a catalyst, urging Miriam to find the courage to reveal the vulnerable sides of herself, to honor the truths she discovered, and to embrace the beauty of her authentic self.

Miriam's real-life encounters with emotional adversity inspired her to immerse herself in understanding the mechanisms of emotional resilience and recovery. Rather than leaning on formal degrees, she honed her understanding through experiential learning, engaging with countless narratives of resilience, and studying various healing modalities from different cultures around the globe.

Motivated by her newfound wisdom and the profound healing she experienced, Miriam felt an unwavering call to share her knowledge with others. Her sincere writings have since served as a beacon, guiding others toward understanding, acceptance, and, ultimately, healing. She leverages her words to empower her readers, encouraging them to reclaim their narratives, find courage amidst chaos, and uncover the power of resilience in their own lives.

Maintaining a disciplined practice of mindful reflection, Miriam also enjoys a life rich in physical wellness and natural exploration. A devotee of Tai Chi, she finds balance and serenity through the practice. The tranquility of nature is her sanctuary, and she relishes any opportunity to explore the world's wonders, often in the joyful company of her beloved cat, Whiskers. Miriam Sutton's profound journey of self-discovery, resilience, and healing continues to inspire readers worldwide.

Printed in Great Britain
by Amazon